DEVELOPMENTAL HANDICAPS
IN BABIES AND YOUNG CHILDREN

DEVELOPMENTAL HANDICAPS IN BABIES AND YOUNG CHILDREN

A Guide for Parents

By

DIANA L. BROWN, ACSW

Chief Social Worker
Mount Carmel Guild Child Study Center
Alhambra Pavilion
Newark, New Jersey

CHARLES C THOMAS • PUBLISHER

Springfield • Illinois • U.S.A.

Published and Distributed Throughout the World by

CHARLES C THOMAS • PUBLISHER

Bannerstone House

301-327 East Lawrence Avenue, Springfield, Illinois, U.S.A.

©1972 by CHARLES C THOMAS • PUBLISHER

ISBN 0-398-02534-7

Library of Congress Catalog Card Number: 72-75911

*With THOMAS BOOKS careful attention is given to all details of
manufacturing and design. It is the Publisher's desire to present books that are
satisfactory as to their physical qualities and artistic possibilities and
appropriate for their particular use. THOMAS BOOKS will be true to those
laws of quality that assure a good name and good will.*

Printed in the United States of America
RN-1

**In memory of
Marge Thorne**

PREFACE

Many families whose babies are developing with difficulty have a sense that "something" is wrong but do not know what the basic problem is, nor do they know what is causing it. As the baby begins to grow and the problem becomes more noticeable (perhaps the baby is slower than others his age, or he does not seem to hear well, or he is always fretful, or he is too quiet), the family may slowly begin to seek professional help. It may take some time before the baby's handicapping condition is diagnosed and even longer before treatment services are found. And the parents get more and more upset.

Having to come to grips with the realization that their baby is suffering from some kind of developmental handicap is heartbreaking for parents. If they do not understand the nature of the handicap, what it means for the child's future and what can be done to help him, they may be unable to get past the crisis.

I have worked with families of handicapped babies for ten years, having started in the same year that President Kennedy announced a great new concern for our country's mentally ill and mentally retarded citizens. In these ten years, much has been learned about the complex relationship between the brain and other systems of the body and about how developmental problems are caused. Many new treatment programs have resulted, with an emphasis on serving babies and young children.

It is my belief that if this information is shared with parents, they can better understand their babies, can know if and when professional help is needed, can handle the initial crisis, and can make better plans for the baby and for the total family.

This book is, then, a result of my work with parents over the years. I have kept in mind the questions they have asked, the experiences they have had, the things they would want to know if they were to start all over again — and the relatively little time busy parents can give to reading.

This very general, nontechnical guide will introduce parents to all aspects of developmental handicaps in babies and young children. It is not concerned with detailed medical, treatment, or counselling information. Rather, it is meant to provide the kinds of basic information which will enable families to get help for their babies and for themselves as soon as possible.

I cannot name all the parents whose experiences, knowledge, wisdom, and encouragement have helped me to write this book. But they will know who they are; and I thank them. Special thanks, too, to the following colleagues who graciously gave me advice and read parts of the manuscript: Morrison S. Levbarg, M.D., F.A.A.P.; Evelyn Pollack, M.A.; Tony Alfano, Ph.D; Harold Friedman, O.D.; Marion Ruminski, M.A.; and Barbara Oldenborg, R.N. They are, however, not responsible for the ways in which I used information they discussed with me.

I am deeply indebted to Sister Lillian Ernest, M.P.F., M.A., my dear friend, colleague, and co-worker, who read the entire manuscript, made many valuable suggestions, and spent many an hour supporting my efforts.

It is difficult to adequately express my gratitude to my family for helping me through all the months of research and writing. My children, Marisa Anne and Gian Arthur, displayed a remarkable understanding of what I was trying to do. Certainly, without the devotion and encouragement of my husband, Arthur, this book could not have been written. It was he who kept the household running on many occasions. He read the manuscript at every stage, made many sound recommendations, and helped with the proof-reading and indexing.

DIANA L. BROWN

CONTENTS

	Page
Preface	vii

Chapter

1. INTRODUCTION 3
   The Handicapped Baby and His family 5
   Early Childhood Development 7
2. WHERE DO HANDICAPS COME FROM? 10
   How Does the Brain Get Damaged? 12
   Things That Do Not Cause Brain Damage 19
3. HOW CAN HANDICAPS IN BABIES BE PREVENTED? 21
4. CHARACTERISTICS OF BRAIN DAMAGE IN BABIES
   AND YOUNG CHILDREN 27
5. GENERAL DEVELOPMENTAL PROBLEMS 31
   Orthopedic Problems 31
   Visual Problems 32
   Hearing Problems 34
   Language and Speech Problems 35
   Minimal Brain Dysfunction 37
6. SOME PRIMARY HANDICAPPING CONDITIONS IN BABIES
   AND YOUNG CHILDREN 40
   Mental Retardation 40
   Mental Illness 44
   Cerebral Palsy 44
   Muscular Dystrophy 45
   Epilepsy 46
   Effects of Lead Poisoning 48
7. WHAT DOES IT ALL MEAN? A SPECIAL DICTIONARY
   FOR PARENTS 50
8. THE DIAGNOSTIC EVALUATION 58
9. SEEKING RESOURCES 69
10. WHAT COUNSELLING IS ALL ABOUT 76

Bibliography 83
Index 87

DEVELOPMENTAL HANDICAPS
IN BABIES AND YOUNG CHILDREN

Chapter 1

INTRODUCTION

W HEN people think about having a baby, it is usually in terms of a healthy, beautiful baby such as we see on television selling diapers or soap or baby food, a baby who gurgles contentedly, is alert and "normal." How many women, as they go along in their pregnancies, have thoughts about their baby being born with something wrong? Just fleeting thoughts, perhaps, because society, of which each of us is a part, doesn't focus on things which are unpleasant or "different."

Only at the time of birth do our hidden fears come out, when we hear ourselves say something like, "My baby, is he all right?" or when we uncover the baby to count his fingers and toes. Books that tell us how to get through a pregnancy or how to have natural childbirth or how to care for a baby go along with the expectation that the baby will be like those babies in the ads. And perhaps that's justified, because about 96 percent of the time it is.

But sometimes it isn't.

Some babies are born with physical or mental problems. The problem can be so mild as to be almost not noticeable; or it can be severe enough, on a very rare occasion, to shake up the hospital staff. Each year in the United States more than 200,000 babies are born with some kind of handicap, defect, or deformity. About 8,200 a year are born with club foot, a relatively minor problem nowadays because it can be corrected. More than 126,000 a year are born mentally retarded. Every year cystic fibrosis occurs in 1 of every 1,000 white babies; sickle cell anemia in 1 of every 500 black babies; Tay-Sachs disease in 1 of every 900 Jewish babies. Out of every 1,000 children sixteen years of age and under, 8 have speech defects and 6 have hearing impairment, because some problems are not noticed in babyhood. While some problems show up at birth, others seem noticeable after a few years, and some come after an illness or accident.

3

Let's look at the word "handicap" for a minute because I shall use it frequently in this book. According to the dictionary, it means any disadvantage or disability or deficiency that restricts or prevents a person from normal achievement. A handicap can be physical or mental. It can affect the person's developmental abilities (functioning, behavior, or appearance) in a way that society considers "different."

Some people use words other than "handicap." They prefer words like "disability" or "impairment" or "exceptional" when talking about a child with a developmental problem. I think the most important thing is that people understand what we mean no matter what word we use. Because it seems to me to have the clearest meaning, I prefer to use the word "handicap." And I will use it to discuss those babies who have developmental problems which can be treated and helped but which are *not* correctable or curable because they are due to some irreversible injury or damage to the brain. The babies I want to talk about are those who often have a combination of mental and physical handicaps and whom we therefore can also correctly refer to as "multiply-handicapped."

Why am I spending so much time explaining what words I will use? Well, it's a fact that youngsters who have a physical problem, but not one that is mentally damaging, have more of society's interest. Since World War II brought home so many young men whose injuries resulted in missing limbs or blindness or deafness, we could not turn our backs on them but promised to help them become part of society again. A smaller, though still significant, number of servicemen came home with psychiatric problems, so interest then developed in their treatment too. But for those others who suffered brain damage and who could not be rehabilitated, there was little said and little done.

And that is reflected in the way we respond to handicapped babies. Since there is presumably no way to make them "normal," many people lose interest in them. We can see, therefore, that it is a little bit different for the family with the handicapped baby than it is for the family with the baby whose physical disability is correctable.

THE HANDICAPPED BABY AND HIS FAMILY

When a baby is born with a physical disability, the family may experience much of the initial upset that the family of the handicapped youngster goes through. But for the family in which the condition will be ongoing, we know that the upset will be more intense, of longer duration, and that there will be certain other special problems to be faced.

However, whether the upset is mild or major, of short duration or for a lifetime, and no matter how much professional interest has been devoted to the child's particular problem, not enough attention has been given to the feelings, the burdens, the pressures of the family.

Where handicaps are concerned, it seems to me that many people, including professionals, either feel the youngster cannot be helped and the parents should give up on him, should somehow not feel for him, and should go on about their lives; or that the parents must accept the child, no matter what, and do certain prescribed things or live in certain prescribed ways because the *only* concern is the child.

In either situation, there is little regard for the variety and complexity of feeling that parents will have and little effort to try to see the child as part of a family, where *everyone's* needs and *everyone's* feelings and *everyone's* rights and *everyone's* strengths and *everyone's* weakenesses can be looked at and evaluated and then a plan worked out that *everyone* in that family can live with.

Several years ago, when I worked in a diagnostic clinic, a couple of my colleagues and I, all childless then, spent a lot of time trying to better understand parents' feelings about having a baby with a developmental problem. We looked at many different kinds of handicaps and tried to decide which, if we had to make a choice, we would pick for our own child. And, of course, we always came up with the same eventual answer: no matter what it was, if it happened to *our* child it would be the worst possible problem.

I mention this only because the experience taught me one of the most important things I've learned in the work that I do: that there is no justification ever for saying to a parent "It could have been worse . . . ." We parents want our children to be normal and healthy. How we react when they are not is a very personal thing.

Other people can show us the possibilities in terms of treatment, or help us to separate fact from fiction, or tell us what *can* be done if we think nothing can be done. And that information may have something, even a lot, to do with how we feel and how we act.

But people deal differently with different kinds of problems. What is a handicap for one family seems not to be for another; what one parent can accept another cannot; what seems possible for one person is impossible for someone else. This is because we are all individuals. And that individuality has to be respected.

What I am saying, really, is that it is important for parents to understand the reality of the problem their baby has and to look at (not be afraid of) and deal with their feelings about it so that they can then make out a plan of action that they think they can follow and live with. The plan should be the best one for themselves, not necessarily the one recommended by the doctor, the grandparents, the neighbors, or well-meaning friends.

How to arrive at that point is the purpose of the pages that follow. What most parents feel they need is information to help them make the necessary decisions. Too often that information is not forthcoming until after the initial crisis is passed.

In ten years of work with families of handicapped youngsters, I have talked to many parents who wished they had known that certain help was available in the community, or that they had understood at the time of crisis what the handicapping condition meant, or that they had had someone to talk to who really knew what was going on.

Parents often feel they are advised to do things by people who know the facts but do not take the time to share them. The parents are then at the mercy of someone else when, in fact, all the information that is known really should be made available to the family so that it can make its own decisions.

An example of what I mean is that parents often have to go along with the latest whims of the professionals. If a baby was born mentally retarded about fifteen or twenty years ago, the parents were generally told to place that baby in an institution, forget him, and go and have another baby right away. Nowadays these same professionals are beginning to advise that such babies remain at home, in the community; and parents are now expected to do the complete opposite of what they used to do, again with little chance to voice objection. And so, it seems, professional opinion may be put above the needs of the family. But if parents are armed with the knowledge to make their *own* decisions, we know from experience that they can make *better* decisions for their families.

Based on the questions parents have asked me, and the information they have sought, I have gathered a lot of general information about the most common developmental problems in babies and very young children. In addition, I have organized a dictionary of many of the terms that parents may hear during the course of their search for help. I have also tried to pull together information which will aid parents who are just beginning their search.

It is my hope that through this effort many more parents will be able to recognize problems if they exist, will reach out for help in the community as soon as they know of the baby's problem, and will thus get help for themselves and for their baby as early as possible.

EARLY CHILDHOOD DEVELOPMENT

Before we talk about babies who are developing slowly, we should perhaps say just a few words about normal physical and mental development. Each baby does develop at his own pace, perhaps later in one area, earlier in another, so that it is not always fair to compare babies. Still, there are some basic things we can look for at certain stages along the way in the first few years; and we use them as a guide in picking up problems that may exist.

Very briefly, then, let's outline the general developmental pattern that is considered to be normal for the pre-school child:

at birth: the baby usually can distinguish light from dark and can hear sounds; he can suck well; he requires complete care and is unaware of the world around him.

1 month: the baby begins to follow objects placed in front of his eyes; he communicates by crying but is beginning to gurgle when he is contented; he may be startled by noises around him; he may begin to smile as he notices familiar faces.

6 months: now the baby begins to really get interested in the world around him; he sits up with support, has good head balance and looks all around; he can smile and laugh and recognize his parents; he begins to roll over and perhaps to crawl; he can hold things in his hand and bring them to his mouth; he gets his first tooth or two; there is a lot of cooing and gurgling.

12 months: the baby can sit well by himself and pull himself to a standing position; he may begin to walk now; he is shy with strangers but happy and playful with his family; he begins to finger-feed himself, to play with the spoon, and to drink from the cup; he begins to imitate sounds, perhaps say "ma-ma" and "da-da", and he understands simple commands and peek-a-boo games.

18 months: he is a small child now, walking well and beginning to run; he plays with his toys by imitating things he sees others do; he tries to undress (pulls off socks, hat, mittens); he feeds himself well with the spoon and holds his cup by himself; he is beginning to show interest in toileting, can respond to simple directions, and can say many simple words and phrases.

2 years: the young child now runs well and can go up stairs one at a time; he plays more purposefully, looks at picture books, and wants to talk about everything; he is completely on table foods and pretty well knows what he wants to eat or not eat; he begins to be interested in listening to music and looking at TV.

3 years: by now the child can feed himself with the fork and is pretty independent at meals; he may be completely day toilet trained and sleep through the night without wetting; he begins to go down stairs one at a time; he begins to dress himself and can entertain himself for a short time; he cuts with scissors, begins to use crayons, and is interested in playing around other children; his speech is clearer, he uses full sentences well; he begins to enjoy and repeat TV commercials, especially musical ones.

4 years: the young child now begins to be independent of his mother, going up and down stairs without help, dressing and undressing (including buttoning and zipping), playing cooperatively with other children; he asks many questions about the world around him (the "why" stage); he is beginning to use his imagination and to count by rote from 1 to 10; he can do little errands and chores around the house; he understands children's programs on TV and can explain them to others. From now on, he moves out to explore his neighborhood and is ready to meet other people who will begin to influence his life.

When a baby seems to be doing things much more slowly than is suggested by the pattern described above, we begin to get concerned that there may be a developmental handicap.

The parents play a most important role in following the baby's early development and in questioning any difficulty they think their baby is having. Even a *feeling* that something is wrong should be discussed with the doctor; many parents can have a sense that there is a problem even if they cannot pinpoint it. It is better to be called an "overanxious parent" than to risk ignoring the early signs of a possible handicap.

Chapter 2

WHERE DO HANDICAPS COME FROM?

W HO are the parents of handicapped babies? In spite of what a lot of people think, we are all the parents of the handicapped in the sense that it can happen to any of us. Parents of handicapped babies are a cross section of our society: married, separated, divorced, unmarried; all races, all religions; under 20 years old to over 40 years old; people who wanted a baby, people who didn't want a baby; rich people, poor people. For some families, the handicapped youngster is the only child, or the first child; in some families, he is one of several children, or perhaps is the youngest child.

How, then, are handicaps caused in babies? While there are many, many cases in which no one really knows the exact cause, there are also many cases in which we do know the cause, or at least what *may* be the cause. Can we predict how or when it will happen, or to whom? Well, let's look a little further into some of the major handicaps and how they seem to happen.

There are many statistics about births, and the ones I use here are quite recent but are only approximations. The current estimate is that about 1 out of every 14 babies born in the United States is born with some kind of birth defect. In the National Health Education Committee's recent list of the twelve major illnesses and diseases in the United States, seven involve central nervous system impairment or brain damage: *mental retardation* (about 126,000 babies a year born with it); *blindness* (over 500,000 legally blind, about 3% of them under age 21); *cerebral palsy* (an estimated 25,000 infants a year born with it); *epilepsy* (close to 4,000,000 people have it in some form); *deafness* (at least 200,000 people totally deaf); *multiple sclerosis* (about 250,000 cases, most occurring in young adulthood); *muscular dystrophy* (about 200,000 cases, nearly two-thirds of them in children between the ages of 3 and 13).

10

These illnesses and diseases are listed, along with arthritis, heart disease, cancer, mental illness, and Parkinsonism (all of which generally affect older adults), as our country's "remaining health problems." All of these problems reach every segment of our society; however, as we will see later, poor people (who suffer, to a much greater degree, *every* problem that society has) seem to bear a disproportionate number of them.

Let us go on, then, to how handicaps occur. We know that the brain controls all the functions of the body. It is the main regulator and coordinator of all the body's activities: it controls our breathing, our thoughts, our feelings, our movements, our learning, our growth. It does all this by receiving "messages" from all the parts of the body and from the world around us, and by sending out "messages" which will make us do the right thing at the right time. (For example, if we need food, our empty stomachs send a message to the brain, and the brain in turn tells us it is time to eat and also tells us how to get the nourishment we need; or if we get near a hot stove, a message is sent to the brain, which then tells us to move away before we get burned.) The "messages" travel through nerve centers in the spinal cord. The combination of the brain and the spinal cord makes up the *central nervous system.*

The brain actually has two halves (called *hemispheres),* each of which controls one side of the body: the right half controls the left side of the body, the left half controls the right side of the body. One hemisphere is usually considered dominant, that is, it controls the eye, arm, hand, leg and foot that a person seems to prefer to use or seems better able to use (for things like looking through a camera, writing, kicking, etc.). Within each half of the brain, different parts of it control different parts of our bodies. The result of any injury or damage to the brain depends, then, on what parts of it are affected.

When brain cells get damaged, they cannot be repaired or regrown (as can bone cells after a broken leg or skin cells after a cut or scrape). It is sometimes true that if brain cells in only the dominant hemisphere are damaged, the same kind of brain cells in the other hemisphere may be trained to take over the same job. A person who has a stroke provides a good example. Let's say the result of the stroke is some damage to the parts in *one* of the hemispheres which control arm and leg movements and speech. The person may become paralyzed on one side and not be able to speak. Rehabilitating that person involves trying to teach the same parts in the *other* hemisphere (those that control arm and leg movements and speech) to take over.

So now we see that if the brain or any of its message centers (nerves) get injured or do not work properly, it will affect our functioning in some way. If there is enough of an injury to some part of the central nervous system, or if particular parts in both hemispheres of the brain are damaged enough, certain handicaps will result. The general term used here to describe all of this is "brain damage."

HOW DOES THE BRAIN GET DAMAGED

There are three basic times when brain damage can occur in a person: before birth, at or during birth, and after birth. We will use these three general headings and look at some of the specific problems which can develop at each of these times. (We will discuss the "hows" but medical science is not yet clear on all the "whys." Also, we do not know why it is that these things will cause problems in some people and not in others.)

Before Birth

This time is also called the "prenatal" period. It is the time while the baby is in the mother's womb. During this time the baby receives his oxygen and his nourishment from his mother through the *placenta* (also called the "afterbirth" at delivery).

Infections in the Mother. These can be viral (such as influenza or rubella), bacterial (such as syphilis), or parasitic (such as toxoplasmosis). When a mother suffers such infections in early pregnancy, the baby she carries can have brain damage, with mental retardation or hearing or visual problems.

Illnesses in the Mother. Illnesses of the pregnant woman, such as kidney disease, high blood pressure, toxemia, or anything which requires medication, surgery, or special medical attention, can be stressful to the baby. Many maternal illnesses will result in damage to the placenta, premature delivery, or an undersized baby.

Irradiation. Women often do not know that there is a danger in receiving x-rays, particularly in the middle area of the body, during pregnancy; the earlier in the pregnancy, the more the danger. There is some concern now about x-rays in the months *before* pregnancy, and people are even beginning to question the possible effect on the baby of x-rays the *father* might have in the months before the baby is conceived.

Attempted Abortion. If a miscarriage does not result from an attempt to abort a baby in any way other than that done by a doctor in a hospital or clinic, the fetus (baby in the womb) may suffer from damage done to the placenta.

Rh Problem. This is a situation in which the mother and the baby have the same blood type but different *Rh* factors in the blood. The mother is Rh-negative and the baby is Rh-positive. The mother's body develops antibodies to the baby's blood; these antibodies pass through the placenta and destroy the baby's red blood cells. The result is an excess amount of a substance in the blood called *bilirubin.* Without treatment, the baby will suffer brain damage or may even die. Fortunately, this problem has recently become preventable and should soon be removed from a list of this kind.

There is a similar condition, in which the mother's blood type is O and the baby's blood type is either A or B. This problem is generally milder than the Rh problem but is still carefully watched in case treatment becomes necessary.

Mother's Age. Very young mothers have a higher incidence of premature deliveries. Older mothers tend to have more difficult first deliveries. Very young mothers (under age 16) and older mothers (over age 40) have a higher percentage of babies born with abnormalities.

Metabolic Disorders. Disorders in the body chemistry of the mother, such as diabetes, sickle cell anemia, or a thyroid condition, can affect the fetus. Many metabolic disorders can be passed from parent to child; some twenty-seven of them have already been identified as leading to mental retardation in the baby.

(Disorders of the body chemistry will result, after birth, in the baby's inability to grow properly. Some examples are (1) phenylketonuria (PKU), in which the body does not produce enough of a certain amino acid necessary to aid in digestion, resulting in brain damage; (2) cystic fibrosis, in which abnormal secretions of the mucous glands result in intestinal problems, poor general growth, and continual upper respiratory infections such as bronchitis and pneumonia; and (3) cretinism, the result of an underactive thyroid gland, leading to slowness in physical and mental development. These are now treatable but there are many other metabolic disorders which still are not.

Chromosome Abnormalities. Chromosomes (found in the body cells) are important because they carry the genes which pass on characteristics and traits from parent to child (heredity). If there is any abnormality in the normal pattern or number of chromosomes, problems can develop in the baby. Sometimes these chromosome differences are known to come from the parent to the baby, and sometimes they just seem to occur by accident while the fetus is being formed.

Microcephaly. This means undersized skull. It may be caused by premature closing of the bones of the skull either before or soon after birth (a condition called *craniostenosis),* or by a lack of growth of the brain.

Hydrocephalus. This is a condition in which there is an accumulation of too much of the fluid which usually circulates around the brain and spinal cord. This extra fluid results either from over-production or because of a blockage which prevents its being absorbed by the body. The result is a separation of the bones of the head and an increase in pressure on the brain. (Hydrocephalus occurs in about 1 out of 500 babies; a good percentage of cases can now be treated surgically.)

Complications of Pregnancy. Examples are *placenta praevia* (in which the placenta is implanted over the opening of the birth canal and may cause bleeding during pregnancy); premature separation of the placenta from the wall of the uterus; toxemia (a metabolic disorder that can occur only in pregnancy and which results in headaches, high blood pressure, fluid retention, etc.); multiple births (twins, triplets, etc.); or any of the illnesses or diseases mentioned earlier. All of these things put great stress on the unborn baby.

Medicines and drugs. Do you remember several years ago when mothers who took thalidomide in early pregnancy began having babies born without arms or legs? Nowadays all medications for pregnant women (even aspirin) are causing concern among doctors. Some medicines *have* to be taken even during pregnancy, and the doctor should always be the person to make the decision as to what medicines a pregnant woman can take; she should not take anything without checking it out with him first.

The narcotic or addictive drugs (such as heroin, morphine, etc.) and hallucinogenic drugs (like LSD) may be causing damage to unborn babies. These drugs are all being studied now and there is some evidence that they may cause chromosome changes in the fetus. Also, many people who take drugs do not eat properly and this can present health problems.

Then there is the question of whether smoking a lot affects the unborn baby. So far, doctors seem to feel that too much smoking may cause premature birth and this, in turn, can cause problems.

Although alcohol may not really be considered as a drug, it can be mentioned here because excess use of alcohol by the mother may cause the same kinds of problems in the baby as does excess use of drugs.

Poor Nutrition. There is evidence that protein deficiency before birth and in the first year after birth can damage a person's mental capacity, for this is the time of the central nervous system's greatest development. Since the mother nourishes the baby during pregnancy, it makes a difference how well or how poorly nourished *she* has been even before she becomes pregnant.

On the other hand, one can get too much of certain vitamins. Not too many years ago it was discovered that too much vitamin D taken during pregnancy could damage the fetus' brain. So, again, the decisions about what is a healthy diet, or what is good nutrition, should really be discussed with a doctor or a nutritionist.

Unknown Causes. There are many things that happen while a baby is developing in the womb that just cannot yet be explained. However, with continued research into the use of metabolic and genetic studies, the time will come when such presently unknown causes will be better understood.

During or At Birth

This time is also called the "natal" period. In this section are the babies who seem to have developed normally during the mother's pregnancy; then something happens at the time of delivery. The result is what some people refer to as "birth injuries."

Prematurity. This is probably the biggest cause of problems at birth. A premature baby is one born before term (the full nine months) or who weighs less than 5 pounds 8 ounces at birth. Because all of the body's systems are usually not fully developed until the nine months of pregnancy have passed, there is a higher chance in "preemies" for physical or mental problems.

Prematurity can be caused by a lot of things, as we've noted earlier: heavy smoking, maternal illness, very young age of mother, multiple births, etc. We have to be very concerned with the toll prematurity takes on babies. For instance, mental retardation is ten times more likely to occur in premature than in full-term infants. And for "preemies" there is about a 50 percent chance of having some kind of developmental problem, ranging from the most minimal neurological impairment to severe mental and physical retardation. In the old days, many premature infants died, but now there is a higher survival rate because of increased medical knowledge.

Most causes of prematurity can be prevented by avoiding the prenatal complications mentioned earlier. Therefore, the concern of parents should be directed toward getting their babies to go to term.

Anoxia. This means lack of oxygen to the brain. Brain damage can occur if for any reason the baby does not get enough oxygen at the time of delivery. Examples are as follows: when the cord is wrapped around the baby's neck; when the mother has toxemia; when the mother has had too much anesthesia during delivery (which slows down the baby's breathing); when labor is prolonged; when the baby has any problem with his lungs which affects his intake of oxygen; or when the baby has convulsions right after birth.

Fetal Position. The normal delivery of the baby from the uterus is "head first." A baby whose delivery position is buttocks first (breech), face up, or shoulder, arm or leg first, has a slightly higher chance of sustaining brain damage. Sometimes these situations may require delivery by caesarian section.

Inadequate Prenatal Care. If the mother is not cared for by a doctor or nurse-midwife during her pregnancy, complications may arise at delivery which might have been avoided or could have been treated or prepared for ahead of time.

Poor Professional Service. This includes all care by the hospital staff. Examples are as follows: inhumane treatment in prenatal clinics (which has the effect of discouraging the mother from coming back routinely); the doctor not coming to the hospital on time; nurses forcing the mother to cross her legs if the doctor is not there yet; a mother delivering in a labor room because there is no one around to know she is ready to deliver; over-medicating the mother; incorrect use of forceps; doing a caesarian section when it is not necessary or hesitating before doing one when it *is* necessary; inadequate nursery care of the newborn. These things happen less often nowadays, and fortunately they are preventable.

Drug-related Withdrawal Symptoms. This condition, which can occur in babies born of drug-addicted (or alcoholic) mothers may result in tremors, hyperactivity, vomiting, fever, convulsions, and coma if the baby is not treated immediately.

Metabolic Disturbances. Any metabolic problem that affects the baby must be observed and treated right after birth in order to correct the imbalances that occur.

Resuscitation of the Newborn. This means causing a just-born baby who is not breathing, or who has stopped breathing, to take a breath. There are now many methods of resuscitating babies who in former times would have died; but some babies may still end up having been without enough oxygen for a long enough period of time to cause brain damage.

After Birth

This time is also called the "postnatal" period.

Encephalitis or Meningitis. These viral illnesses cause inflammation of the brain, or the membrane around the brain, and can therefore damage it.

Regular Measles (Rubeola). Once considered a harmless childhood disease, we now know that it can lead to serious complications (in about 1 out of 1,000 cases) such as pneumonia or measles encephalitis; and the child can end up with mental retardation, behavioral problems, visual problems, or loss of hearing.

Fortunately a vaccine against this disease, which has been available since 1963, causes lifetime immunity. Many parents do not realize the importance of measles vaccination and so the disease has not yet been wiped out. Since most of the cases occur in preschool age children, the vaccination should be given no later than age 2 and preferably at age 1.

(This disease should not be confused with German measles, also called rubella, which is a mild disease in children but can be dangerous for the fetus of the pregnant woman. By vaccinating children with the new rubella vaccine, we really are trying to protect future unborn babies by wiping out the disease altogether.)

Trauma. This means a severe physical or emotional injury which can result in damage to, or dysfunction of, the brain. Examples would be a bad fall on (or blow to) the head; an extremely frightening, painful, or upsetting experience; severe burns; infection of the brain or central nervous system; or a growth in the brain such as a tumor.

Poor Nutrition. We've already mentioned that during the first year of life, protein deficiency can cause damage to the brain and can affect general physical growth.

Ingestion of Poisons. We have all heard stories about babies eating or drinking poisonous things like household cleaners, poisonous plants, and medicines. Thousands of children are injured each year, and hundreds die. Many children live but suffer from brain damage.

One of the most common kinds of poisoning in very young children is lead poisoning, occurring when the child eats lead-based paint from furniture or from the walls.

Convulsive Disorder. Seizures in a very young child, particularly in an infant (under 2 years of age), and particularly if repeated (that is, not controlled by medication), can cause brain damage.

Cerebral Palsy. This is a problem with motor ability and muscle coordination that is related to damage of the brain at birth.

Congenital Heart Defect. If a baby's heart is not functioning properly he may have difficulty getting enough oxygen circulated through his body. Depending on the kind of heart defect and the extent of the problem of carrying oxygen to all parts of the body, brain damage and, of course, even death, can result.

Antibiotics and Other Medications. Since the discovery of many lifesaving medications, people who otherwise would have died are now being kept alive. Part of our population is handicapped, and now more of them are given longer lives because of better medical care. Also, some people whose lives are saved through modern medical techniques survive with brain damage.

Population Growth. As the population of the world increases, and as the number of births increase, the *percentage* of people with handicaps may remain constant but the *actual number* increases.

Child Abuse. An abused child is one who is purposely physically or mentally injured or neglected by a parent figure. For very small children, the term "battered baby" has been used. Injuries inflicted by the parent may result in brain damage or even death for the child.

This is a very important social problem today since it is estimated that *at least* 10,000 children a year are abused, and 1 out of 4 dies of his injuries. It is of course a completely preventable problem and one in which all of us can be involved. Every person has an obligation to protect any child who seems to be abused. A call to the local police department or child welfare agency should be made even in a suspicious case. The person who makes such a call is protected by law so there is no reason to fear getting involved.

THINGS THAT DO NOT CAUSE BRAIN DAMAGE

Just a few words about the fact that many times parents think they did things during the period of pregnancy that might have caused the baby harm, when in fact they did not. Some common misconceptions are as follows:

Ordinary Falls. It is very hard to damage the fetus if the mother has a fall in which she does not get seriously hurt. The baby is quite well protected by the amniotic fluid (the sack of waters that stays around him in the uterus until he is born).

Sexual Intercourse Late in Pregnancy. There is no evidence that sexual relations can injure the fetus. However, once labor has started there *is* a danger of infection to the baby and so, at that time, there should not be any sexual relations.

Being Around A Handicapped Person. Some people think that if the mother looks at, or is around, a person with a deformity or a handicap, it will affect the unborn baby. This is simply not true; it can have no effect on the baby.

Brain Damaged People Have Brain Damaged Babies. Unless there is an hereditary disease involved (one that passes through the genes from generation to generation), there is no reason for a brain damaged person to give birth to a brain damaged baby.

Emotional Upset. Although doctors are always interested in how a woman feels during pregnancy because how she feels may affect her eating and sleeping habits and her general health, an emotional upset *by itself* does not hurt the unborn baby.

Consanguinity. This means to be related to your husband or wife by blood, e.g. first cousins, uncle and niece, aunt and nephew. There *is* concern about the children from this kind of union *only* if there is some hereditary disease in the family.

Chapter 3

HOW CAN HANDICAPS IN BABIES BE PREVENTED?

ONE of the best ways to deal with handicaps is to try to prevent the kinds of things we have been talking about so far. That is not as hard as it sounds. Let's look at some of the preventions that are available.

Better Maternal and Infant Care

One of the best ways to insure a healthy baby is for the mother to see a doctor as soon as she thinks she is pregnant and to continue to see him or a nurse-midwife on a monthly basis until the baby is born. In this way any problems that develop can be corrected, questions the mother may have can be answered, and everyone can be sure that there are no unsolvable problems at delivery.

Babies, after birth, should be followed monthly by a well-baby clinic or a private doctor, at least through the first year. Not only can the doctor watch the baby's general development, but he can give all the vaccinations and shots necessary to protect the baby from certain diseases. The mother can also check with the doctor or his staff if the baby is having any sleeping or feeding problems or seems in any way different from normal.

Earlier Diagnosis of Problems

Obviously, if the baby does have a problem, the earlier doctors know about it, the quicker treatment can be started. If certain illnesses are caught before they are really serious, some problems can be avoided entirely.

Parent Awareness

If a parent knows what to look for in the way of signs of illness or indications of some problem in development, that parent is in a much better position to prevent certain problems or at least to get help for them as soon as possible. In order to know what is unusual, parents should not only have some idea of what normal development is like for a youngster of up to three or four years of age, but should also have some basic knowledge of what kinds of things might hint that the baby is sick and needs medical care. Still the best general rule-of-thumb book available, in my opinion, is Doctor Benjamin Spock's famous book, *Baby and Child Care* (published by Pocket Books, New York).

Continued Medical and Behavioral Research.

One by one, many of the world's medical problems are being resolved in terms of cure and prevention. Researchers need money, so one way to help them is to give financial support to one of the many valuable research programs in this country. If you know someone with a certain problem, you can support a research program in that special area and encourage all your relatives and friends to do the same.

If your child has one of the problems that is still being studied, making yourself available to answer questions or allowing your child to try new treatments are some things you may want to consider.

Don't underestimate the importance of research for the future even if your child cannot be helped. It is estimated that by 1975 there will be 75,000,000 school-age children in America, and 12,000,000 of them will have some kind of developmental problem (3,000,000 of them will have some degree of mental retardation). We are talking, as President John F. Kennedy said, of "our most precious asset — our children," the adult generation of tomorrow.

Amniocentesis

This is a relatively new procedure, which involves withdrawing some amniotic fluid from the pregnant mother's womb for chemical and chromosomal analysis. It is done if there is reason to believe the mother may be carrying a baby with some kind of defect. "Intrauterine diagnosis" or "prenatal diagnosis" are other terms used for this procedure.

Amniocentesis, a relatively painless process done in a few hours' stay at a hospital, can often uncover a problem in a baby in time either for some curative treatment to be started (as in the Rh problem) or for the parents to decide whether to have an abortion performed (in the case of a defect being present). Mothers who have been exposed to rubella, who have an Rh problem, who have already given birth to a child with a handicap, or who know they carry some hereditary problem, may easily have amniocentesis done.

New Medical Treatments

Every day there are breakthroughs in medical research and new treatments for conditions that were previously untreatable. Examples of these are genetic counselling before pregnancy if hereditary problems are known to exist, treatment of the Rh-negative mother, the special diet for infants with phenylketonuria (PKU), and the new drugs that seem to relieve the symptoms of muscular dystrophy. Sometimes parents are not aware that there is treatment available for a particular condition — treatment that could prevent a possible problem or that could at least make a great deal of difference in the child's functioning.

Adequate Medical Care at Delivery

Most hospitals now have a pediatrician available at the delivery so that he can take immediate and complete care of the baby as soon as it is born, allowing the doctor who delivers the baby to continue looking after the mother. In this way, if the baby is showing any signs of difficulty, there is a specialist right there to go into immediate action.

There are certain problems that can be picked up immediately after birth by doing some blood or urine studies on the newborn. (In many states now, the very simple test to detect PKU is given routinely to every newborn, even though the condition may show up in only 1 out of 10,000 babies.)

The Apgar Score is a procedure developed by Dr. Virginia Apgar which measures five vital signs at birth and again soon after birth. Number values are given by the doctor to the baby's heart rate, breathing, muscle tone, reflexes, and skin color. The score for each can be 0 to 2; a perfect total score is 10. A total score below 7 indicates the possibility of some problem later on and may even mean that the baby is not doing well and needs some form of treatment immediately. In most hospitals, doing an Apgar is standard procedure, and the score should be available to the parents.

Eliminating Pollution

We do not yet know the extent of pollution's dangers. But we *can* say that bad air, bad water, and too much noise do affect people's general health and may cause an increase in certain diseases. Poor health in a parent can add risk for the offspring.

Eliminating Poverty

When we talk about prevention of handicaps, we cannot avoid facing one of our most serious social problems — that of poverty. Recently a classic study of poverty in New Jersey as a causal factor in mental retardation made clear that the poor suffer just about every one of the problems we have discussed so far, and they therefore also suffer the highest number of babies born with handicaps.

One of the major causes of brain damage is poor nutrition. The poor cannot get enough of the right kinds of foods. About 20 million Americans suffer from malnutrition. What does it mean for a country to have a large number of malnourished people who may suffer from brain damage? We can look to a recent tragedy for the answer.

In 1969, during the war between Nigeria and Biafra, the Biafran civilian population was literally starved on a large scale. Many thousands of babies died, and those who managed to survive will be mentally retarded because it is too late now to try to undo the brain damage by feeding them. What will Biafra be like in about twenty-five years, with an adult population that is going to have an unusually high percentage of mental retardates?

What about the living conditions of the poor? They have worse, more crowded, less hygienic living conditions. Therefore, babies and small children are more exposed to diseases of infancy and childhood such as colds, pneumonia, measles, encephalitis, etc. The children have to play in the roads or streets, dodging traffic, and are more likely to suffer trauma due to accidents (such as getting hit by cars).

In cold areas, there may be insufficient heat and not enough heavy clothing. With many people sharing the same living quarters, the children may not get enough rest, may have lower resistance to disease, and may be more exposed to infections and illnesses. Since old tenement houses are more likely to have many layers of lead-based paint on the walls, the incidence of lead poisoning is quite high among poor people who live in them.

Let's look, too, at the health care the poor receive. Since they tend to have more illness and disease, it would seem logical that they would need the most and the best health services. But just the opposite is true. The ratio of private physicians to patients in large urban areas or in farm areas where migrant workers live is much lower than in suburban areas. Therefore many poor people have to depend on hospital emergency rooms and clinics for their routine medical care. That means long waits in crowded rooms, doctors who are strangers and who may not speak the same language as the patient, inadequate examinations due to the pressure of time. In the cold of winter, with few cars available and taxis almost nonexistent during the night hours, many poor people who are sick cannot get to a hospital. Even if a person is *very* sick, ambulances do not come too quickly.

Illnesses which might be minor if treated right away often become serious or acute. Babies and small children, as we have said, are exposed to more diseases and get less medication with which to treat them.

Poor women, who until quite recently did not have access to birth control information, are more likely than their middle-class sisters to be very young for their first pregnancy, to have more pregnancies, to have them closer together, and to go on having them until a later age.

We know the connection between very young mothers, or older mothers, and prematurity and brain damage. We know that having many pregnancies close together can affect general health; and we know the connection between poor general health and prematurity and brain damage. Until very recently (and now in only a few states), the poor did not have access to abortions by competent doctors; and we know the connection between attempted abortion and brain damage.

Many poor women work and cannot afford to sit for hours in a clinic. Or they have no one to leave with their other young or ill children in order to get to the prenatal clinic. They therefore may not keep up with routine appointments in either the prenatal or (later on) well-baby clinics. We know the connection between poor prenatal care and brain damage; and we know the connection between poor general medical follow-up in babies and brain damage.

Perhaps I've made my point. However, even for those only concerned with more concrete things, like dollars and cents, let me add that the estimated cost *per year* in the United States for care of brain damaged people is about $550,000,000. And if you estimate the number of handicapped individuals who are involved, it is close to 8,000,000 people, or a group about the size of the population of New York City!

The toll in *human* costs is incalculable. Let us keep in mind that about 50 percent of a person's basic ability is developed before he gets to the general public's attention by entering school. So if we are to make any significant progress in changing the statistics by lessening the number of youngsters who suffer from the results of brain damage, we have got to get to them in those first four or five years of their lives.

In order to find them, the public — that means you, me, and everyone around us — must learn to look for signs of developmental problems in babies and small children. We must know how and where help can be found. And we must encourage parents to get help for their handicapped babies.

Chapter 4

CHARACTERISTICS OF BRAIN DAMAGE
IN BABIES AND YOUNG CHILDREN

IN this and the next two chapters, I would like to give a bit of general information about some of the major handicapping conditions that can be found in babies and very young children. We have been talking so much about brain damage that perhaps first we should look again at what we mean by those two words and then at how we can learn to recognize brain damage in babies as early as possible.

As we noted earlier, we use the term "brain damage" when we believe that the brain for some reason is not functioning at its highest level because of some physical or emotional injury to it or to the nerve centers in the spinal cord. Where babies are concerned, the result of brain damage is usually a combination of mental and physical developmental problems. There are many words used that can mean the same thing; some of them are "chronic brain syndrome," "central nervous system impairment," "central nervous system dysfunction," "organic brain damage," or "organic impairment."

When we use the term "brain damage" here, then, we will assume it relates to a baby or young child who is functioning below the level of intelligence expected for his age, and who gives evidence of having difficulty sending or receiving "messages" through the central nervous system.

Besides the more obvious signs of handicap in babies and young children, such as slow mental development or physical disabilities, there are certain behavioral characteristics that seem to be common to brain damaged youngsters. The degrees to which a child shows them can vary; and not all brain damaged youngsters will show every one of them.

You will note that each of these characteristics is also found in *non*-brain damaged youngsters at certain ages. Brain damaged children will show them, however, beyond the "normal" times and to a much greater degree or intensity.

It is important to remember that these behaviors are not planned on the child's part and he cannot easily control them. In some instances he may not even be aware of them.

Hyperactivity

Hyperactivity means excessive, purposeless, often uncontrollable discharges of energy. The hyperactive child seems to have endless energy, to never sleep or even sit down. He exhausts his parents in their efforts to keep up with him.

Distractibility

The distractible child seems unable to concentrate on, or to perform, any activity for even a short period of time. Any noise, any person walking by, any thought that comes into his mind, can take the child away from the thing he is doing or trying to do. The distractible child is so easily stimulated by the things around him that he can go from one thing to another literally every minute.

Impulsiveness

This is, really, unpredictable behavior. The child seems to do things without paying attention to what the result will be or even to why he is doing them. If the child gets an urge to scream, to run, to hug, to throw, to sing, to cry, etc., he does it because he has difficulty controlling his impulses.

Irritability

This is noted when the child seems more fretful than the situation warrants. He may be easily annoyed, go into a tantrum over something that seems relatively minor. Loud noises, crowded places, being rushed, going to new places or meeting new people, all of these may upset him. Even changes in his daily routine can change his mood. He seems to have little frustration tolerance;

that is, he has little patience when things do not go his way, and "his way" can change from one minute to the next.

Awkwardness

Very often the child seems to have poor coordination. He is clumsy, may trip a lot, or may have trouble sitting, standing, walking, running, or jumping. When reaching for things, he may over-reach and miss them; or he may grab things and then drop them right away. There are many different ways that awkwardness shows up, depending on the age of the child.

Aggressiveness

The aggressive child is one who has an excessive, or exaggerated, degree of anger that is usually directed toward another person. Since the child may become irritable for no obvious reason (as noted above), his aggression may not be understood or expected. It may really be related to his irritability or his impulsiveness.

Destructiveness

This is similar to aggressiveness but it is usually the *result* of the aggression. Often destructiveness seems to be an aimless kind of anger that is directed at a *thing* rather than at a person. In small children, the "thing" is often a toy or some object that the child can touch with his hands. Sometimes the child may turn his destructiveness to himself (what we call "self-destructive behavior"); that is, he may scratch or bite himself, pull at his hair or clothes, or bang his head against a wall or the side of his crib.

Immaturity

Immaturity means that the child is functioning socially or developmentally below his chronological age (the level we would expect him to be functioning at for the number of years he has been alive). Even a child who is basically of normal intelligence may be immature in the way that he acts.

Perseveration

The perseverative child may be repetitive in what he does or what he says, in a way that is not purposeful or useful. He may persist in an activity even when asked to go on to something else. He may play with a toy in a consistent but unmeaningful way. He may repeat a sound or a word over and over so that it loses its meaning or intent.

Sometimes it is very hard to "break into" a child's perseveration; we may get him to stop one perseverative behavior only to see him go on to a new one.

Poor Speech

Although not really a *behavioral* problem, we mention poor speech here because of its importance in the diagnosis of brain damage. Speech difficulties are often the first "sign" that parents of brain damaged youngsters really notice.

Poor speech would include any kind of unclear, garbled, or immature speech (and would also include, of course, lack of speech).

Almost all brain damaged youngsters have delays in speech development, but this does *not* mean that all youngsters who have delayed speech are brain damaged.

Chapter 5

GENERAL DEVELOPMENTAL PROBLEMS

As a baby grows, our first clues to his handicapping condition are usually his difficulties or delays in the developmental milestones. Some of these difficulties are easier to detect than others; some are noticed earlier than others; and each of them affects the others.

Because all the areas of development are so interrelated, it is hard to discuss *problem* areas in separate categories. We do so in the following arbitrary way only so that each one can be understood more clearly and discussed in some detail.

ORTHOPEDIC PROBLEMS

Orthopedic problems are generally defined as those physical conditions which interfere with the functioning of the bones, muscles, or joints. It is almost impossible to quote meaningful statistics about the incidence of orthopedic problems in the population because people differ on how severe the problem must be in order to be counted as a statistic.

We are concerned here with those orthopedic problems which are considered to have been present from birth and which are generally part of a multiply-handicapping condition (that is, a combination of physical and mental handicaps). They can vary from a very minor thing such as flat feet to the complete inability to use the arms, legs, or body. In between are such things as cleft palate and harelip, spina bifida, congenital heart disease, hydrocephalus, extra fingers and toes, missing arms or legs, congenital hip dislocations, bone diseases or deformities, or the muscular problems connected with cerebral palsy or muscular dystrophy.

Orthopedic problems in babies can result from many of the things which cause brain damage and which were discussed in Chapter 2. Examples would be maternal illnesses, genetic

31

problems, birth injuries, and so on.

These orthopedic problems affect the baby's ability to use his hands, arms, feet, legs, and body, and to coordinate what he sees and hears with the movements of his body. *Any* problems the baby seems to be having in the use of his body or arms or legs should be reported to a doctor. Many of them can be treated so that the child's general functioning can be improved.

VISUAL PROBLEMS

Because it is hard to clarify how different investigators define "visual problems," it is very loosely estimated that more than 500,000 people in the United States are *legally blind* and that between 3 percent to 10 percent of them are under the age of 21. *Legal blindness* means (1) total blindness; (2) vision of 20/200 or less in the better eye with glasses (that is, at a distance of 20 feet the person can read something that a person with no visual problem can read at 200 feet distance); or (3) a field of vision so restricted that the person can only see a small area at a time.

At least 1,000,000 people in the United States are *functionally blind* (that is, sight is better than 20/200 but the person is unable to read ordinary newspaper print without glasses). Around 4 million other people have permanent and noncorrectable eye problems.

The National Society for Prevention of Blindness estimates that 1 of every 4 children in the United States needs some form of eye care.

Many causes of visual problems in babies are not known. And the known causes have changed in recent years. It used to be, in the early 1900's, that babies were often blinded at birth from an infectious organism found in the birth canal of the mother. This was called "babies' sore eye" (or *ophthalmia neonatorum*). It was discovered that a drop of silver nitrate put into each eye right after birth could prevent this kind of blindness. Since these drops are now automatically given to every newborn, "babies' sore eye" is no longer a problem.

Babies who contracted syphilis while in the mother's womb were also frequently born blind. However, with all mothers who get prenatal care being screened for syphilis (and treated when necessary), this is not the major problem it used to be.

In the 1940's and 1950's, there was a significant increase in blindness in premature babies. It was discovered that this condition, called *retrolental fibroplasia,* was actually caused by prolonged exposure of the babies to the very high levels of oxygen in the incubators. Since this was causing more than 50 percent of the blindness in babies, the discovery of the cause was of great importance; nowadays cases of *retrolental fibroplasia* are rare.

We tend now to see few cases of total blindness or severe visual problems in non-brain damaged babies. Instead, babies who have very poor vision may have been affected by diseases or illnesses such as measles, whooping cough, scarlet fever, lead poisoning, meningitis or encephalitis; or may have been exposed before birth to rubella, syphilis, toxoplasmosis or other infections. These youngsters, therefore, often have other handicaps besides poor vision. For instance, "rubella babies" may have cataracts (generally more common in older adults) plus hearing problems or mental retardation.

Vision, of course, can also be affected by severe burns, substances in the eye, or injury directly to the eye or optic nerve.

The visually handicapped baby is likely to make slower than average progress in the first couple of years of life. This does not mean the baby is necessarily mentally retarded; however, his progress should be followed carefully. Extra stimulation and extra encouragement are necessary for the baby. Extra patience is necessary on the parents' part. The baby will need many, many experiences in hearing, touching, smelling, and moving around, and the parents must be sure to provide them.

Sometimes parents are not certain that their baby has a visual problem; they may think he is just a very quiet baby. Therefore, it is very important that all babies and small children receive regular eye checkups. Undiagnosed eye problems can affect other areas of development and can cause things like speech and emotional problems.

In the small baby of about 6 months of age, one of the most important warning signs is one eye turning in or out. It means that one eye is weaker than the other; that the eyes are not working together; and that the stronger eye is doing most of the seeing. Sight can be lost in the weaker eye if it is not treated. This condition is commonly called "lazy eye"; the medical term for it is *amblyopia.* Some people feel it is normal for an infant's eyes to wander or turn and that the condition will take care of itself in time. However, the chances are slim that the baby will outgrow it; and certainly it should not be happening by the time the baby has begun motor activities such as crawling and sitting.

Parents should discuss with a doctor a baby's seeming inability to follow a moving person or toy with his eyes. With small children, warning signs of possible visual problems might also be red or swollen eyes, much rubbing of the eyes, frowning or squinting, tilting the head when looking at things, or complaints of headache or nausea that have no physical cause.

Brain damaged babies should be checked especially carefully. However, *any* youngster who seems to have *any* developmental problem should be checked to be sure that lack of vision is not the cause. Obviously, the earlier a visual problem can be diagnosed, the better the treatment can be and the less the chance of other developmental or emotional problems arising.

HEARING PROBLEMS

Hearing loss is considered a major handicapping condition because of its affect on the development of language and speech. Since there is no large-scale screening of infants for hearing problems, the statistics vary from a low of 2 percent to a high of 20 percent of small children in the United States who suffer from hearing problems.

Since only a very small percentage of young children with hearing loss have *no* response to sound, early detection and early treatment of hearing problems are extremely important. Hearing loss can vary from very mild to profound (deafness). The causes are many and not all are clearly understood as yet. Some things which might cause hearing problems are genetic abnormalities, chronic upper respiratory infections, or other of the problems before, at, or after birth which were discussed in Chapter 2.

There are two basic kinds of hearing loss: *conductive,* affecting the transmission of sound from the outside world through the outer and middle ear; and *sensorineural,* affecting the inner ear or auditory nerves (those nerves that have to do with hearing).

In addition to those with true hearing loss, there are children whose hearing is not actually impaired but who are unable to distinguish between certain sounds or are unable to understand the speech that they hear. There are also children with psychological (emotional) problems, such as the autistic child, who may "shut out" the sounds around them and who will not respond to them.

Even in the absence of any known or suspected cause for a possible hearing problem, infants and very young children should be examined (1) if they fail to respond to sounds around them, such as human voices, ringing bells, or handclapping (rather than noises which transmit vibrations and can be *felt,* such as slamming doors or windows); (2) if they do not continue babbling in the second half of the first year of life after having cooed or babbled in the first few months; or (3) if they do not develop speech and do not respond when people speak to them.

We focus so much on hearing loss and lack of speech because the two are very closely connected. A child cannot naturally learn verbal communication skills (understanding and using speech) unless he hears speech around him. The older a child is before he develops these skills, the harder it will be for him to develop them. Therefore, difficulty in communication due to hearing loss can be minimized, or perhaps even prevented, if the hearing problem is discovered and treated as early as possible.

LANGUAGE AND SPEECH PROBLEMS

No exact figures are available on the number of children in the United States who have language or speech problems. However, speech difficulties are the most common of all handicapping conditions because so many other handicaps affect speech development.

Language and speech are not the same thing. Since even professionals have some disagreement about the meanings of these two words, we will use them here in the following way: *language* can be verbal (spoken) or nonverbal (gestures) communication;

speech is meaningful verbal language.

A child can have difficulty understanding or using either language or speech or both. For example, the infant can often make the sound "ma-ma," but he begins to make that sound because it gives him a nice feeling within his mouth or because he may like the way it sounds. It is quite a while, around one year of age, before he begins to associate that sound with the person who seems to respond the most to it; thus she becomes "ma-ma." The child then goes on to learn to understand and use words (and eventually sentences) which represent actions, persons, things, ideas, or feelings.

We begin to be concerned about language and speech problems when a baby or small child does not have the normal, or average, pattern of speech development. In order to know what are problems, then, we must know what the normal pattern is. Let us look at that pattern, according to the child's age:

8 − 10 months: the baby begins to understand and to recognize gestures, tones of voice, single words, and short phrases. His chief means of communication, however, is still crying (when in distress) and gurgling (when happy), both of which he has learned to use because of the way people have responded to them.

1 year: the baby begins to understand and to imitate certain sounds he hears other people make; as people respond to them in certain ways, he uses them again and again until he "learns" them ("bye-bye," "go," "no," "ma-ma," "da-da").

2 years: by now, the child uses verbal language in order to explore the world around him; he points to things and learns to name them ("book," "milk," "cup") and to describe them ("big," "bad," "more milk," "good boy").

3 years: the child now begins to really use speech well; he can ask questions and demand answers from others; this is often called the "why" stage.

By age 3 1/2 or 4 years, the child is able to give and receive information pretty well. He uses sentences, and his speech is more like that of a grown-up and less like that of a baby. Pronunciation of certain sounds, however, may not yet be fully developed.

The causes of language and speech problems can be physical (due to brain injury or brain damage from any of the causes mentioned in Chapter 2) or emotional (as with the autistic child, who has the physical ability to develop language and speech but who does not communicate because of emotional problems). Whatever the reason, speech therapy will probably be necessary to help the child in this important area of development.

MINIMAL BRAIN DYSFUNCTION

Although it is not an actual developmental problem, we include a section on minimal brain dysfunction because if it is not diagnosed and treated in the early years, the child may develop behavioral, language, speech, learning, or emotional problems. Therefore, a child who is basically of normal intelligence may eventually function on a mentally retarded level.

Children with minimal brain dysfunction (MBD hereafter) are also referred to as "brain injured," "neurologically impaired," "dyslexic," "perceptually impaired" or as having "learning disabilities." They all mean essentially the same thing: that the child, because of some improper working of the brain or other parts of the central nervous system, has difficulty understanding and responding to the world around him. Basically MBD is an educational (learning) problem rather than a medical one. The child's behavior and his difficulty with learning mark him as "different" from the average child.

The MBD child's problems are mainly in the areas that have to do with understanding or using spoken or written language. This would include listening, thinking, speaking, reading, writing, spelling, and arithmetic.

Until a few years ago, MBD was not known as a problem; children who had MBD symptoms used to be called "slow learners," "lazy," "behavior problems," and so on. Even now, many cases are not picked up until school age. The minimal estimate of the incidence of MBD is about 5 percent of our nation's children. With special treatment and special education in the early years, MBD children should be able to get through school and have normal lives.

MBD children generally have what we call perceptual problems, that is, they have trouble organizing and interpreting the "messages" that the outside world sends to the brain through the eyes and ears. As a result of these perceptual problems, the children may respond inappropriately. They may have poor judgment about size, space, shapes, directions, etc. They may have trouble sifting out sounds or things that they see, or controlling impulses that they have. The MBD child may be able to see only the general things around him and not be able to focus on one item; or he may *only* be able to focus on one thing at a time and miss "the overall picture." He may seem to have no fear of dangerous situations; or he may be extremely fearful of the most ordinary situations.

MBD children may have trouble remembering things, and they may have problems in paying attention and in following commands. Walking, running, jumping, buttoning, throwing or catching a ball, all may be very hard for these children.

Emotional problems can develop (1) because the child experiences failure so many times and in so many ways; (2) because of the distorted ways in which he perceives the world; and (3) because of the ways in which people react to him as a result of his behavior problems. MBD children may exhibit some or all of the behavioral characteristics of brain damage that we discussed in Chapter 4. One of the greatest of these behavior problems is the MBD child's excessive hyperactivity. Strangely enough, in his infancy he may be *underactive,* but around 2 or 3 years of age, the hyperactivity begins.

Although MBD may be caused in the same ways that other brain damaging conditions are caused, it is really very hard to diagnose because the signs of it are so subtle. Often there is no *medical* evidence that the central nervous system is not functioning properly. There may or may not be what are called "positive signs" in a neurological examination or from an electroencephalogram (EEG). Sometimes the only evidence comes through formal psychological or speech evaluations, or by observing the child's performance and behavior in a group of children his own age.

Because most small children do not have special evaluations until school age (and then generally only if the teacher feels the need for them because the child is having some learning or behavior problem), MBD is often not diagnosed until the child is 5 or 6 years old. Fortunately, however, more and more professional people, particularly nursery school personnel and medical doctors, are becoming aware of MBD symptoms and are referring preschool age children who show some of the signs for complete diagnostic work-ups and special preschool treatment programs.

Chapter 6

SOME PRIMARY HANDICAPPING CONDITIONS IN BABIES AND YOUNG CHILDREN

Handicapped babies and young children may need many different kinds of special services because of their multiple handicaps. However, they are usually serviced according to their major, or primary, difficulty. Let us look at some of the most common primary handicapping conditions, then, keeping in mind that a particular child may seem to fit in more than one of the following categories.

MENTAL RETARDATION

We discuss mental retardation first for many reasons. First of all, it is the single largest childhood medical problem in the United States. Although not a disease in itself, it is a condition that results from many causes.

About 3 percent of the population in America is considered to have mental retardation in some form. The Report of the President's Panel to Combat Mental Retardation states that mental retardation affects twice as many individuals as blindness, polio, cerebral palsy, and rheumatic heart disease combined; 10 times as many as diabetes; 20 times as many as tuberculosis; and 25 times as many as muscular dystrophy.

There are only four diseases which occur with more frequency than mental retardation: mental illness, heart disease, arthritis, and cancer. However, these four diseases all tend to occur later in life (that is, to the *adult* population).

An estimated 15 million to 20 million families in America have a mentally retarded member. By 1970 there were more than 6 1/2 million mental retardates in the United States, 3 million of them

40

under the age of 20. It has been reported that a mentally retarded baby is born every 5 minutes, or about 300 times a day. Often the mental retardation accompanies some physical handicap.

Do these figures seem impossibly high? Well, that may be because fortunately about 90 percent of the mentally retarded fall into what we call the mildly retarded range, and they are able to become a part of the "normal" population at some point during their lifetimes. We are really talking in this book about the other 10 percent, the group whose mental retardation becomes noticeable to the people around them while they are still in the preschool years (that is, under the age of 5).

Definition

There are many definitions of mental retardation. In its simplest form, we can think of the mentally retarded youngster as one who has trouble learning and in applying what he does learn to everyday living. The definition of the American Association on Mental Deficiency is that mental retardation "refers to sub-average general intellectual functioning which originated during the developmental period and is associated with impairment in adaptive behavior." "Adaptive behavior" in *preschoolers* refers to developmental milestones, and "impairment" shows up as a lag in motor activities such as crawling, sitting, walking, eating, and communication skills. In *school-age* children "adaptive behavior" refers to learning, and "impairment" shows up in difficulties in learning and using academic skills. In *adults* "adaptive behavior" refers to social adjustment, and "impairment" shows up in problems of independent living or in being unable to meet the community's requirements in terms of work, marriage, parenthood, etc.

Categories of Mental Retardation

Often when we think of a mentally retarded youngster, we think of someone who is "hopeless" or who can't do anything. However, mental retardation can range from very mild to profound. The more retarded a child is, the more chance that he will also have physical handicaps, since his brain damage will be more severe.

There are four general classifications of mental retardation, according to level of functioning. They are as follows:

Mild	IQ 50 – 75	Educable
Moderate	IQ 35 – 50	Trainable
Severe	IQ 20 – 35	Non-trainable
Profound	IQ 0 – 20	Custodial

Since a "normal" level of functioning is considered to start with IQ 90, the group of people who function between IQ 75 and IQ 90 are generally considered to be "borderline"; however, they are generally maintained, if possible, in the regular classes in school so we will not discuss them here.

Mild Retardation

As we mentioned earlier, the mildly retarded are about 90 percent of the mentally retarded population or more than 2 1/2 million children (that is, people under the age of 20). Since their main problem is in the area of learning, these youngsters may not even be diagnosed as mentally retarded until they start school. They attend *educable* special classes in school. They may learn many academic skills but because of their slower development they learn at a slower-than-normal rate.

As the IQ scores tell us, mildly retarded youngsters function at a level that is from about one-half to three-quarters of the average, or "normal," child. As they grow into adulthood, mildly retarded people can usually be trained to work in the community and to live pretty independent lives. They thus "pass" back into normal society after they get out of high school.

Because their retardation shows up mainly in the academic learning areas, mildly retarded youngsters are often referred to as "six-hour retardates" (the school day being about six hours).

Moderate Retardation

Moderately retarded youngsters number over 150,000 in the American population, or about 5 percent of the mentally retarded population.) They are usually diagnosed in the preschool years. According to their IQ scores, they function from about one-quarter to one-half of the level of the average child. They develop slowly in all areas and almost always have problems in learning to talk.

(Moderately retarded youngsters attend *trainable* special education classes in school, where the main focus is on learning self-care and socialization. Some trainable children do learn to read and write a bit. These children, as they grow to adulthood, can be trained to work at jobs in sheltered workshops rather than out in the business world (although, again, some trainable retardates *do* move into jobs in the community). They need to have supervision all their lives; therefore, they cannot live alone.)

Severe and Profound Retardation

(The severely retarded are about 3 1/2 percent of the mentally retarded population, or somewhere around 100,000 in number. The profoundly retarded are about 1 1/2 percent, or around 50,000 in number. They are usually diagnosed as mentally retarded in infancy, often right at birth. There are often noticeable physical handicaps in these babies.)

(According to their IQ scores, these children function, at best, up to about one-quarter of the level of the average child. They generally do not attend school, although some severely retarded youngsters do attend the *trainable* special education classes. Their development is very, very slow, and often these youngsters do not learn to speak well.)

Training of severely and profoundly retarded youngsters is geared to self-care, although they generally require assistance in all areas of general daily living. Some severely retarded adults can work in sheltered workshops, but most do not.

(The profoundly retarded generally are so extremely slow in developing, and so unaware of the world around them, that very little can be done in terms of training them. Many of the profoundly mentally retarded are also very physically retarded. It is often hard to care for them at home since they require round-the-clock nursing care and supervision. They constitute most of the more than 200,000 mental retardates who live in institutions.)

MENTAL ILLNESS (AUTISM)

Many people think of the mentally retarded as "crazy" or mentally ill. This is not so. However, it *is* true that a mentally retarded person *may* become mentally ill and that a mentally ill person *may seem to be* mentally retarded. The autistic, or mentally ill, young child does often function as a mental retardate; and sometimes the primary diagnosis is very hard to make.

Mental illness refers to personality and behavior disorders which involve the emotions and which are often temporary (and curable) conditions. Generally, mental illness occurs in older children and adults after a period of relatively normal development. The person's functioning is changed because his *emotions,* or very strong feelings, interfere with his "normal" responses.

There are, however, some babies who seem to have these emotional problems right from birth, and they are diagnosed as suffering from *infantile autism.* These babies seem to be withdrawn from the world around them. Their behavior stays at the infant's level in many cases; it is as if they do not want to grow up.

The actual cause of infantile autism is not really known. Some doctors feel it has an organic basis (perhaps some disturbance in the body chemistry); others think that it is caused by a deep problem in the mother-baby relationship; still others think that it is a combination of the two. These autistic children are felt to have basically normal intellectual potential. Treatment is therefore different for the mentally ill child than for the mentally retarded child. It is very important that the diagnosis be made as carefully and as accurately as possible.

CEREBRAL PALSY

Cerebral palsy is a condition caused by damage to the brain either before or at birth. It is characterized by a lack of control over the muscles of the body. There are three main types of cerebral palsy: (1) *spastic,* in which the person moves stiffly and with difficulty; (2) *athetoid,* in which the person has involuntary and uncontrolled movements; and (3) *ataxic,* in which the person's sense of balance and depth perception are disturbed.

In general, cerebral palsy is the result of certain problems with the muscle control centers of the brain. Depending on the location and extent of the brain damage, the results can include lack of balance, tremors (trembling or "shaking"), spasms (alternate contracting and relaxing of muscles), seizures, difficulty in walking, poor speech, poor control of face muscles, problems in seeing and hearing, and mental retardation.

Since cerebral palsy occurs most often at birth, we assume that means that the cause may be insufficient oxygen to the infant's brain during the birth process. Also, since it occurs most often at birth, we know that it is neither hereditary nor contagious, but rather an accident of nature. In the United States some 25,000 babies a year are born with cerebral palsy. Although there is no cure for it, there *is* treatment at special "CP centers" across the country.

The degree of cerebral palsy can range from so mild that it is almost not noticeable, to very severe. About 50 percent to 70 percent of cerebral palsied youngsters have mental retardation to some degree; and about 30 percent of them have seizure disorders. Many have speech problems, as well as hearing and visual problems; therefore, children with cerebral palsy are considered to be "multiply-handicapped."

Early diagnosis of cerebral palsy is very important in terms of treatment. Parents should therefore be concerned and consult their doctor if the baby has trouble in feeding (sucking or swallowing), in developing muscular control, or in showing interest in the things around him.

MUSCULAR DYSTROPHY

Muscular dystrophy is, as its name implies, a disease of the muscles. It is what is called a *chronic disease,* one that steadily progresses over a long period of time and for which there is no cure.

Although the exact cause of muscular dystrophy is not known, it is thought to be a genetic problem (a hereditary disease) which seems to be sex-linked in that it tends to show up in the male but is passed on through the female. This disease may begin to show itself in early childhood. Actually there are four different types of muscular dystrophy, but the two most common ones are also the ones which occur in early childhood: those known as the *Duchenne* type and the *Juvenile* type.

Babies who have muscular problems do not necessarily have muscular dystrophy. However, any difficulty in muscle tone should be checked out by a doctor. There should be particular concern if the baby seems markedly less active than the average, if his balance is poor, if he falls a lot or has trouble holding his head up or sitting or walking, if he tires very easily, or if he seems to be generally weak.

Diagnosis of muscular dystrophy is made by chemical examination of muscle tissue (in a hospital). Treatment at the present time is mainly physical therapy, exercise programs, and continuing medical care to reduce the possibilities of respiratory infections which are a complication of the disease. Very recently there has been much experimental work done with drugs which might, in the future, reverse some of the symptoms of muscular dystrophy.

EPILEPSY

Epilepsy, which comes from the Greek word for "seizure," is not a disease but a symptom of some kind of irritation of the brain. It results from an excessive discharge of nervous or electrical energy in the brain. The exact way that these energy discharges occur is not known.

According to the Epilepsy Foundation of America, 1 child out of 50 in the United States suffers from epilepsy in some form. This disorder is considered to be chronic in that most people who have it are susceptible to seizures for a long time, perhaps a lifetime, even if they do not actually have seizures all the time.

The form that these abnormal energy discharges, or seizures, takes can vary. A lot seems to depend on the area in the brain where the discharges are coming from. The most familiar form is *convulsion* (see below). About 80 percent of the children with epilepsy can have their seizures at least partially controlled with medication; many of them can get complete control. Medications that are used to treat seizures are called *anticonvulsants.*

Not only do we not know exactly how seizures occur, but in most cases we do not even know why. We *do* know, however, that when babies and very small children have seizures, they are either caused by a very high fever (and called *febrile convulsions*) or because of brain damage or brain injury. (In the older child or adult, epilepsy can also be caused by brain injury or brain damage resulting from illnesses like encephalitis or such things as brain hemorrhages or tumors. In most cases, though, the cause is not known and the person has what is called *ideopathic epilepsy.*)

Some people have seizures frequently, perhaps several in a day; others may only have a few seizures in a lifetime. The medical specialist who knows the most about seizures is a neurologist, and one of his basic diagnostic tools is the electroencephalogram (EEG), which is a test that records the electrical discharges in the brain.

There are two main kinds of seizures that babies and preschool children may have. They are called grand mal and petit mal.

Grand Mal. These seizures are the most common and the most noticeable. They are also called *convulsions.* What we see is a violent shaking of the entire body which usually lasts for a few minutes (although on rare occasions it can go on for an hour or more). There are spasms all over the body. The child's face may turn bluish; there may be saliva coming out of the mouth. Unconsciousness, or a deep sleep, usually follows. When he wakes up, the child usually does not remember anything about the seizure. Four out of five children with epilepsy, or about 80 percent, have grand mal seizures.

Petit Mal. These seizures are often very hard for the average person to detect. They are not convulsions but show up as slight lapses in consciousness. They may seem to be "staring spells" or "daydreaming." Sometimes all that shows is a flickering of the eyelids or a twitching of the mouth. These seizures usually last only a few seconds; but they may occur repeatedly, many times in a day. Petit mal seizures are most common in young children and often disappear by adolescence. About 30 percent of epileptic children have petit mal seizures; but many of them will also have grand mal seizures.

I do want to add a word about *febrile convulsions.* About one-third of all childhood seizures are, or start out as, febrile convulsions; that is, they are triggered by a high fever. They occur mostly in very small children, between the ages of 6 months to 4 or 5 years. Some youngsters have febrile convulsions if their fever goes way up to 105 or 106 degrees; some have them with a lower fever.

Since seizures in infants are very serious because they may cause brain damage, it is extremely important that a doctor be consulted if a baby has a febrile convulsion. Although there is no definite relationship between seizures and mental retardation, we do know that mental retardation *can* result if brain damage in a baby or very young child is caused by continued and severe seizures.

EFFECTS OF LEAD POISONING

The medical term for this condition is *plumbism.* We give extra attention to lead poisoning because it is a condition which is entirely preventable. Although not a condition resulting from brain damage, we discuss it here because it is such a major cause of brain damage in small children, yet it is often not even diagnosed until the signs of brain damage are obvious.

It is estimated that there are more than 400,000 young children in the United States today with dangerous lead levels in their blood; 93 percent of the known cases occur in children between the ages of 1 and 4 years, and 85 percent in children between the ages of 1 and 3 years.

Lead poisoning is caused by ingesting (eating or breathing) anything that has lead in it; the most common way is eating chips of lead-based paint. Since lead-based paint (which has been illegal in house paint since World War II) is often still found on the inner layers of walls of old houses, and since poor people tend to live more often in very old and dilapidated tenement housing, there are many cases of lead poisoning found among the poor.

Or so it has been up to now. Very recently, the New York City Bureau of Lead Poisoning Control found that about 10 percent of all household paints on sale in the city of New York contained more than the legal limit of lead!

Since a few chips a day, over a period of a few months, can begin to cause brain damage, and since children under the age of 4 years are more likely than older children to eat things other than food, the risk is great if there is any lead-based paint on the walls or furniture of any home where small children spend a lot of time.

The *symptoms* of lead poisoning are vomiting, frequent stomachaches, poor appetite, nervousness, irritability, sudden clumsiness when walking, and possibly bluish gums. The *results* of lead poisoning can be tiny brain hemorrhages (causing brain damage), convulsions, blindness, paralysis in the arms or legs, coma, and (if the damage is severe enough) death.

Many people interested in trying to eliminate lead poisoning would like to see all young children tested for it. In that way, as many cases as possible could be diagnosed before the symptoms occur and the poisoning could be stopped before brain damage results.

In January, 1971, President Nixon signed a bill into law which authorized the allocation, for the year 1971, of more than $25,000,000 to help fight lead poisoning in the United States. By August, 1971, only $2,000,000 of the money had been appropriated by Congress. New York City alone spends over $2,000,000 a year just for casefinding and inspection work!

The screening test for lead poisoning is very simple. It involves a sample of blood taken from the child. This can be done in a hospital, in a clinic, or in a doctor's office. The blood is then chemically tested for the level of lead in it.

Chapter 7

WHAT DOES IT ALL MEAN?
A SPECIAL DICTIONARY FOR PARENTS

MANY people who work in the field of the handicapped often forget that most people do not understand the meaning of many of the specialized words that we use. Many parents either do not get a chance to ask, or are reluctant to ask, about things they do not understand.

I have gathered here as many of the words that we use as I could think of, so that when parents take a youngster for a diagnostic work-up or for special treatment, they can have some good idea of what is going on.

Abortion — the ending of a pregnancy before the twenty-fourth week; it can be spontaneous (occurs by itself) or induced (brought on intentionally).

Amino acids — the end products of protein digestion; they are necessary for tissue repair and growth. If for some reason there is a breakdown in this digestive process, it can be detected through what is called an *amino acid screening.*

Amniocentesis — the withdrawal from the pregnant mother's womb of some amniotic fluid (usually between the fourteenth and eighteenth weeks of pregnancy) in order to chemically analyze cells from the baby. It is used to try to prevent handicaps by treating Rh problems and by allowing abortions of those fetuses which are discovered to be abnormal. It can also help parents who are afraid to take a chance that their baby might be born with some defect that is in their families. Because a chromosome study is part of this procedure, amniocentesis can also incidentally tell the sex of the baby before birth.

Amniotic fluid — the liquid, or "bag of waters" that surrounds the baby while it is in the mother's uterus (womb). Skin cells of the baby are sloughed off into the amniotic fluid and they are what are studied in amniocentesis.

Anomaly — anything unusual or irregular or different from the general rule. It

50

usually refers to some physical characteristic; a congenital anomaly is one that happens to a baby before he is born and that is diagnosed at birth.

Anoxia — the result of a decreased or insufficient amount of oxygen in the organs and tissues of the body. An anoxic person lacks enough oxygen, may turn purplish or bluish, and seems to struggle for air if conscious. Anoxia at the time of birth is a major cause of brain damage in babies.

Apgar score — a scale devised by Dr. Virginia Apgar to measure a newborn baby's vital signs at birth and right after birth.

Aphasia — a disorder of language learning; the loss of the ability to express or understand language symbols (the spoken or written word) as a result of some central nervous system dysfunction. It can be *expressive* (or "motor"), in which the person can understand but cannot give back appropriate responses; *receptive* (or "sensory"), in which the person cannot understand language he hears or sees; or both. *Congenital aphasia* means language did not develop at all, rather than that it was once developed and then lost.

Ataxia — muscle incoordination that shows itself, during a purposeful movement, by irregularity and lack of precision. It is often seen in people with cerebral palsy.

Athetoid — constant slow, writhing, involuntary movements, usually of a part of an arm or leg (or hand or foot), that stops only during sleep. It is often found in people with cerebral palsy.

Autism — refers to mental illness in babies or young children. Sometimes called *infantile autism,* it is really childhood schizophrenia. The child either stays at, or goes back to, his infancy in terms of his behavior; and he seems to withdraw from the world around him.

Behavior modification — a theory of changing behavior by understanding and manipulating the external (from the world around him) social or behavioral forces that operate on a person. The belief is that a person is likely to repeat behavior that is followed by a pleasant, or gratifying, experience. The emphasis is therefore on giving positive reinforcements (rewards) for desirable behavior, while ignoring as much as possible undesirable behavior. This method is called *operant conditioning.*

Brain — the large, soft mass of tissue located inside the skull. It is the primary center for regulating and coordinating all body activities. It is also the center of awareness, thought, memory, reason, judgment, and feeling. Different parts of the brain control different things; therefore, the result of brain injury or brain damage depends on which part or parts of the brain are affected.

Brain damage — the result of injury to, or lack of development of, brain cells. It can also be called *brain injury.*

Breech delivery — when a baby is born feet first or buttocks first. It occurs in about 1 out of 60 deliveries.

Central nervous system — part of the total nervous system. It includes the brain and the spinal cord. (The nerve endings and fibers that go from the brain and spinal cord to all the parts of the body are called the *peripheral nervous system.*)

Cerebral palsy — also referred to as "C.P.," it describes a defect of, or difficulty in, motor power and coordination that is related to damage of the brain at birth.

Chromosome — a microscopic part of the cell, containing thousands of genes (hereditary determiners, or traits that are passed from parents to their children). In humans, the normal number of chromosomes in each cell is 46 (or 23 pairs, including the sex chromosomes that determine whether a person will be a male or a female); one of each pair comes from each parent. If the total number or pattern of chromosomes differs for any reason, the baby can have certain diseases or defects.

A chromosome study is sometimes done on a baby to help diagnose a suspected condition; and sometimes it is done on parents to see if they are carriers of an inheritable disease. A chromosome study is done through a special kind of examination of cells obtained through a blood sample. *Karyotype* is another name for chromosome study, and it is a "picture" of the chromosomes arranged in pairs according to size and shape.

Chronological age — sometimes referred to as *C.A.,* it means the actual numbers of years of a person's life at any given time.

Coma — an abnormally deep sleep, or state of unconsciousness, in which the person cannot be aroused (awakened). It may be due to injury to the head affecting the brain; to the effects of certain drugs or poisons; or to central nervous system illness or disease.

Congenital — any mental or physical trait or condition that exists at birth because of something that happened to the fetus during the time it was in the womb; it may or may not be hereditary.

Cranium — the skull; the bones of the head that are around the brain.

Cyanosis — the dark purple or bluish color of the skin and mucous membranes due to lack of oxygen (and too much carbon dioxide) in the blood; or due to a severe reduction of blood moving through the body (very poor circulation).

Cystic fibrosis — a congenital metabolic disorder in which the body gives off certain abnormal secretions that are carried throughout the body in the blood. Symptoms usually appear in early childhood. The disease is chronic and degenerative, with no known cure. It is usually found only in white people.

Diagnosis — the determination, after evaluation of the symptoms available, of the nature of a disease or condition; the decision as to what the condition really is.

Dyslexia — a reading disability; an impairment, usually due to central nervous system dysfunction, that has to do with printed symbols. It is the most common of the learning disabilities. It is estimated that between 3 and 7 percent of the population of the United States has some dyslexia; boys seem to outnumber girls almost 3 to 1.

The dyslexic child often sees letters or numbers reversed (this is normal in children of a certain age but then passes); he may not be able to tell differences between words he hears that sound somewhat alike; he may have problems with directions (left, right, up, down); he may have problems with size and shape discriminations (big, small, a square, a circle). All of these things affect the ability to learn to read.

ECG (or EKG) — stands for *electrocardiogram;* a "picture" of the heart action which results from a machine recording of the electrical currents originating in the heart.

Echolalia — the involuntary repetition of a word or phrase just spoken by another person.

Echopraxia — the imitation of an action of another person.

EEG — stands for *electroencephalogram;* a record resulting from the use of a special machine to measure the electrical discharges of the brain. It is a painless examination in which electrodes from the machine are attached to the head with dabs of a glue-like substance. This examination, sometimes referred to as a "brain wave test," is often used as part of the diagnostic evaluation of a child suspected of having brain injury, brain damage, or epilepsy.

Encephalitis — an inflammation of the brain, usually caused by an infection. *Secondary encephalitis* is that which results from a disease or illness (such as measles or mumps encephalitis). Encephalitis is sometimes referred to as *sleeping sickness.*

Encephalopathy — a general term for any disease of the brain.

Enzyme — a substance in the body capable of causing chemical changes in other substances (food, for instance), without itself being changed. Enzymes are found particularly in the digestive juices, causing substances in food to break down into simpler compounds so the body can use them. Each enzyme can only work on one particular compound. The more common ones break down fats, starches, proteins, and sugar. The end products are *amino acids.*

Etiology — the cause of an illness, disease, or condition.

Fetus — what the baby is called before birth and while it is in the mother's uterus (womb).

Gait — the way one walks. Many brain damaged children have what is called an "awkward gait."

Galactosemia — a metabolic disorder, starting in infancy, in which there are abnormal amounts of the enzyme *galactose* in the blood. The result can be physical and mental retardation, enlargement of the liver and spleen, and cataracts.

Genes — those parts of the body cell which hold the characteristics that parents pass on to their children (heredity). Genes are located on the chromosomes. A *dominant gene* is one that is inherited from both parents and that usually is visible in the child; a *recessive gene* is one that is inherited from one parent and the chances of it being seen in the child are less.

　　Examples of what genes control are hair, eye, and skin color; height; certain disease conditions or tendencies toward them (such as hemophilia, sickle cell anemia, enzyme disorders, diabetes); and perhaps certain talents or behaviors.

Gestation — the period of pregnancy; the time from when the baby is conceived (conception) to delivery (birth). The "normal", or average, gestation is 280 days, or about nine months.

Heredity — the characteristics, conditions, or traits which are passed down in a family from parents to children.

I.Q. — stands for *intelligence quotient;* an index or measurement of a person's mental age, determined through the use of standard psychological tests. I.Q. scores between 90 and 110 are considered average, or "normal."

Intelligence test — also called *psychological test;* a way of measuring the difference between people, or between the reactions of the same person on different occasions. It is used to determine the person's I.Q.

Language disorder — any problem in using symbols for communication; therefore, it can be a problem in speaking, writing, or reading.

Meningitis — inflammation of the membranes around the brain or spinal cord.

Mental age — sometimes referred to as *M.A.,* it is the age of a person "mentally" as opposed to his chronological age. It is determined through the use of psychological tests. It establishes the age at which the person's level of achievement is, no matter how many years old he actually is.

Mental illness — any disorder which affects the mind or behavior in such a way that the person acts peculiar, bizarre, or different from what society considers "normal"; and which affects a person's daily functioning. In the old days, someone who was mentally ill was called "insane." The specialist who treats mental illness is a psychiatrist.

Metabolic disorder — a problem in tissue change, that is, in the chemical changes of the body which result from converting food into body energy.

This kind of disorder is caused by some abnormality in enzyme production.

Mongolism — probably the most commonly recognized form of mental retardation. It is a condition caused by a chromosome problem and it results in physical and mental retardation.

For young mothers the chances of having a mongoloid youngster are about 1 out of 2000; the chance increases with age, until over 35, when the possibility is about 1 out of 50. The name comes from the oriental look of the eyes; however, the medical term is *Down's syndrome.* There are several "signs" of mongolism that doctors use in making the diagnosis; confirmation of it is often made with a chromosome study.

Neonate — the newborn baby up to 28 days of age.

Nerves — bundles of fibers which transmit impulses or "messages" from one part of the body to another.

Patterning — a method of training in which constantly repeated exercises are used in an effort to get other, healthy brain cells to take over the functioning of damaged brain cells. This method is practiced by the Institutes for the Achievement of Human Potential (headquarters in Philadelphia) and is also known as the "Doman-Delacato method."

Pica — a hunger to eat things that are not edible (things other than food).

PKU — stands for *phenylketonuria,* a congenital metabolic disorder in which there are abnormal amounts of the enzyme *phenylalanine* in the blood, resulting in brain damage. This condition is now treated with a special diet.

Pneumoencephalogram — an x-ray picture of the brain taken by replacing the cerebrospinal fluid with air or gas. It is sometimes used to help diagnose brain injury, brain damage, or a tumor.

Postmaturity — when pregnancy goes well beyond term. A postmature baby begins to lose weight and can begin to suffer from anoxia.

Prematurity — when pregnancy ends before the ninth month. A premature baby weighs less than 5 pounds 8 ounces at birth.

Prenatal — before birth.

Prognosis — a forecast of the probable course or outcome of a particular illness, disease, or condition.

Psychotherapy — a method of treatment of emotional disorders. It is based primarily on verbal (talking) or nonverbal (playing) communication, rather than on drug therapy or shock therapy.

Resuscitation — the stimulation of the breathing center in a person's brain to get the person breathing or breathing better.

Sickle cell anemia — a genetic disease in which the red blood cells change to a shape resembling a sickle. These red blood cells then reduce the amount of oxygen going through the body, thus slowly causing damage to various parts of the body. It occurs mostly in black people. Although the symptoms may be treated, this disease is considered chronic and degenerative because there is no known cure.

S.Q. — stands for *social quotient*. It is an index of a person's ability to look after his own needs and to take responsibility for himself. It gives the age, therefore, at which the person is functioning *socially* (his social age) rather than how many years old he actually is.

Spasms — alternate contracting and relaxing of muscles.

Spastic — the state of such increased muscle tone that there is exaggeration of all the reflexes. It is often found in people with cerebral palsy.

Specialist — the person who deals with a particular problem area. Examples of the kinds of specialists the handicapped youngster and his parents may meet are as follows:

audiologist — the person who is trained to evaluate, diagnose, and treat hearing problems in children.

endocrinologist — the medical doctor who specializes in the hormonal (glandular) system.

geneticist — the medical doctor who studies chromosomes and genes, who performs amniocentesis, and who counsels people about the risk of producing babies with certain genetic problems.

neurologist — the medical doctor whose area is neurological problems, or problems of the central nervous system.

neurosurgeon — the medical doctor who specializes in performing operations that have to do with the central nervous system.

nutritionist — the person who is trained especially in the use of food for growth and general health.

obstetrician — the medical doctor who specializes in delivering babies and in treating diseases specific to women.

ophthalmologist— the medical doctor whose specialty is in problems or diseases of the eye or vision, and including performing eye surgery.

optometrist — the specialist in the scientific examination of the eyes to diagnose disease, and to treat vision problems through the use of lenses (glasses) or exercises but *not* through medication or surgery.

orthopedist — the medical doctor who treats all disabilities or diseases that have to do with the bones, the joints, and certain deformities of the body.

otologist — the medical doctor who specializes in diagnosis and treatment of ear problems.

pediatrician — the medical doctor whose specialty is the general medical care of children (generally those under the age of 12 years).

physiatrist — the medical doctor who specializes in rehabilitation through other than surgical means.

physical therapist — the person skilled and specially trained in treatment of the body by massage or exercise, as prescribed by the physiatrist.

psychiatrist — the medical doctor who specializes in the treatment of mental illness and emotional disturbance.

psychoanalyst — a specialist in treatment of mentally ill or emotionally disturbed people; his professional degree (educational background) may be medical, or he may be a certified psychologist or social worker.

psychologist — the person who is trained and certified to administer intelligence tests and who can also evaluate and treat people with emotional problems.

public health nurse — the registered nurse who is community-based and who is specially trained to deal with community health problems, or health problems in the home.

social worker — the person who is trained and certified to diagnose and treat social problems in the individual or in the family; and to work directly in the community for the improvement of social conditions which interfere with the mental and physical health of all people.

speech pathologist — the person who is trained and certified to evaluate, diagnose, and treat speech and language problems.

Spinal tap — a laboratory procedure in which fluid is withdrawn from the spinal canal for diagnostic purposes.

Syndrome — a group or set of symptoms that together make up a certain disease or condition. A common example is mongolism, or Down's syndrome. *Chronic brain syndrome* is a term used to refer to a nonspecific disturbance of brain function that is of long duration.

Tay-Sachs disease — a genetic disease that affects the central nervous system and that leads to death in early childhood. It is found only in people of Jewish ancestry.

Toxoplasmosis — a parasitic infection which often goes undiagnosed but is reportedly carried by 500 million human beings all over the world. It is generally contracted through eating raw meat or through exposure to fecal matter from cats.

Trauma — a serious physical or emotional injury.

Chapter 8

THE DIAGNOSTIC EVALUATION

N OW that you have a pretty good idea about the meanings of the terms you would hear when a child is being evaluated, let's go on to the how's and why's of having a child receive a complete diagnostic work-up.

Generally, when a parent suspects something is wrong with the child, the pediatrician or family doctor is the first person consulted. What evaluations follow depends very much on that first doctor's recommendations. Sometimes a family is referred to several different specialists for certain specific examinations; or a diagnostic center may be recommended.

There are many advantages to going to a diagnostic center for a complete work-up of a child suspected of having developmental problems.

The first one is the convenience for the family; all evaluations can be done at one place which the family and the child can become familiar with.

Secondly, all possible specialists, with the most up-to-date knowledge, are available for consultation (particularly if the diagnostic center is hospital- or university-affiliated).

Thirdly, it is usually cheaper than going to several specialists individually and privately. Most private specialists have set fees whereas diagnostic centers usually scale the evaluations according to family income.

Fourthly, all the specialists who see the child in a diagnostic center can get together to go over their individual impressions and recommendations so that they can exchange ideas and can together come up with a pretty thorough and accurate picture of the child's abilities and difficulties. They can then recommend a comprehensive treatment program based on the latest research and specialized training of the staff.

Lastly, a diagnostic center is more likely to have available a wide variety of follow-up services for the child and his family for as long as they need special services.

It may be helpful to outline what a general diagnostic evaluation would probably consist of at a center such as I have been talking about. Parents who are looking for services can then have a guide to help them decide what kinds of evaluations are most applicable to their own needs.

At diagnostic centers the whole key to the service is the idea of the *diagnostic team.* The team members are people from various disciplines (or professions) who have chosen to work together and who have a mutual respect for each other's area of specialization. They know that the only way to really understand the child they are evaluating is to know, as well as possible, every area of his functioning and to see him as part of a family unit. Further, in order to help the family work out the best kind of treatment plan for the *total* family, they must know the parents and other important members of the family as well as possible too.

Let's look, now, at who the members of the diagnostic team are, and what kinds of evaluations they do.

Intake Interview and Social History

Generally, the first contact is made with the social worker, who is the member of the team who screens requests for evaluations. This is to insure that the family is at the right kind of diagnostic facility. If the request seems appropriate, an intake interview is scheduled for the parents so that they can visit the center, ask questions about the evaluation (what it involves, how much it will cost, how long it will take, etc.) and share with the social worker as much as they know about the child's difficulties and the reason they are asking for help at this particular time.

A social history is then taken. The parents are asked to tell as much as they can remember about the mother's pregnancy and delivery; the child's development (age of sitting, standing, walking, feeding, toilet training, etc.); the type of handicap and its severity; and what the child's problem means to the family.

It is important for the center to know how long the parents have felt the child has been having difficulty (did it start right at birth, or later on?) and what kinds of stresses have been put on the family by the child's special needs. The social worker can then get a picture of how the child is functioning in the family and in the world around him, and also how the total family is managing.

The social worker coordinates the evaluation process and follows the case until the work-up is completed. If other agencies in the community are involved (nursery school, private doctors, hospitals, etc.), the social worker is available to arrange exchanges of information if the parents are agreeable to it. If the parents have any questions about what is going on, or about problems with appointments, or any upset about the evaluation or the diagnosis, or whatever, the social worker should be there to smooth the way as much as possible. While the primary concern of the other team members is the *child,* the primary concern of the social worker is the *total family unit.*

When counselling is indicated for the parents or other members of the family, the social worker is one of the team members who is qualified to serve as counsellor. Counselling may be individual or group, according to each family's needs and the amount of staff time available.

Physical Examination

The initial part of the medical work-up involves a complete physical examination by a pediatrician in order to get an idea of the child's general health at the time of evaluation and to note any physical defects that are present.

The parents may be asked to review the child's medical history from the time of birth, including any special medications the child may have taken.

The child will be undressed so that all parts of his body may be examined. How he stands and walks are observed. His height and weight are taken as are measurements of the head, chest, and abdomen. His reflexes are tested. Then the body is carefully examined for any abnormalities. This is literally a head-to-toe evaluation. The pediatrician checks the child's hair, eyes, nose, throat, ears, neck, heart, chest, abdomen, liver, spleen, skin, arms, legs, hands, and feet. This is done to rule out disease and also to seek any clues to explain the child's problem in functioning. Essentially, then, the team pediatrician gives the kind of thorough check-up that the child's own doctor has given him at some time before.

Part of the physical examination also involves laboratory work-up: a complete blood count, urinalysis, amino acid screening, and perhaps a chromosome study. There are also routine x-rays of the skull, chest, and wrist bones (this last measures bone age). Again, these are done to screen out any possible illnesses or diseases or to give clues to the basic problem.

If any special medical problem is suspected, such as an hormonal imbalance, a heart problem, an orthopedic problem, or such, a consultation is arranged with the medical doctor who specializes in that particular area. He may do further tests and recommend certain treatment.

Neurological Evaluation

Since many brain damaged youngsters have central nervous system impairment of some degree, they are often seen by the neurologist to get a more specific understanding of just what neurological problems exist. The neurologist tests the finer reflexes, checks into any history of seizures, and may be involved in any decision about medication for the child who has seizures or is hyperactive.

It is the neurologist who may order an electroencephalogram (EEG) and who reads the results of it. The neurologist can often determine the extent of the brain damage, what parts of the brain are affected, and whether seizures are or will be part of the overall problem.

Psychological Evaluation

The purpose of psychological testing is to classify the child according to his general ability (that is, the things he can and cannot do, the things he does or does not know).

Although such testing is used mostly in school systems in order to evaluate children for different levels of instruction, preschool children who have some difficulty in functioning are also tested.

In this way, the particular areas of difficulty can be pinpointed and the exact level that the child is functioning at can be determined.

The scores that result from various tests give a picture of the child's performance. For instance, certain tests measure intellectual performance and give a score which is called the *intelligence quotient* (IQ); others measure social performance and give a score which is called the *social quotient* (SQ).

For children who function at least at the three-year level and who show some signs of having emotional problems, *projective tests* may be given. These tests do not have specific "correct" answers, as do the intelligence tests, but they evaluate the child's emotional responses to given pictures or situations. (The best known projective test is the Rorschach, or "ink-blot" test.)

There are many different kinds of psychological tests. We will discuss here only those which are used for preschool children. These tests are called *diagnostic tests* because they are designed to look at the child's performance and to give information about the causes of his difficulties. There are special tests for deaf and blind children and for children who cannot talk. In the future there will be tests for children with severe motor handicaps because psychologists are always working to find new and better ways to evaluate people with special problems.

All tests for infants and preschool youngsters are *individual* tests in that one psychologist administers the tests to one child at a time. There are special tests for the infant group (age birth to 18 months); and for the preschool group (age 18 months to 5 years). They are performance tests, in which written or spoken language usually is not required in the instructions, the test items, or the answers. For infants, the best-known test is the Cattell Intelligence Scale; for preschoolers, the Merrill-Palmer Scale.

The Vineland Social Maturity Scale, which is administered to the parent rather than to the child, measures the child's ability to take care of his personal needs and to take certain kinds of responsibility. In this test the parents are simply asked questions about the child.

The Vineland Scale covers ages from birth to 25 years, but it is mostly used with very young children and brain damaged children.

The scores that are given, called the *social quotient* (SQ) and *social age* (SA) usually approximate the intelligence quotient (IQ) and mental age (MA) obtained from other tests. Some of the items on the Vineland Scale that concern small children have to do with general self-help: eating, dressing, toileting, communicating, and getting along with others.

Psychiatric Evaluation

This evaluation is really directed at the child and his family. The parents of a preschool child are probably the most important people in his life and will be connected with any emotional problems he may have. All children, whether or not they have problems, will react in certain ways to their parents and their parents to them.

Children who are brain damaged may or may not have emotional problems. Parents of brain damaged youngsters may be very upset by the diagnosis and may not be sure how to handle the child. So the psychiatrist talks to the parents and plays with (or talks to) the child to get an idea of how the total family is dealing with the child's handicap.

Seeing the psychiatrist does not in any way mean that the family is "sick" or "disturbed" or "crazy" or anything like that. The psychiatrist is concerned with how the parents *feel;* how they are managing with the crisis of the child's problems; what their concerns are for the future; what the child's handicap means to them and to their other children; and how he, the psychiatrist, can help them to be less upset and confused if that is the case.

The psychiatrist can also prescribe medications which are used in the treatment of emotional problems.

Since many families *are* upset but are afraid or ashamed to ask for help for their child or for themselves, a routine psychiatric evaluation gives every family member the chance to talk out his feelings and to get help if that seems to be needed. And if a very young child is showing signs of emotional problems, it may be best to work through the parents to change that child's behavior.

Hearing Evaluation

Most brain damaged youngsters have problems in the area of

developing language and speech. Since one thing that may affect the ability to speak is how well one hears, the child's hearing should always be checked to insure that there is not a hearing problem which is preventing the child from learning to speak. If a hearing problem is diagnosed, the child should immediately be treated medically (if possible) or fitted with hearing aids. (Hearing aids can even be worn in infancy.)

The person who does the hearing evaluation is an audiologist. This evaluation involves an interview with the parents regarding the child's developmental and medical history; an evaluation of the child's behavior during the interview; and actual hearing tests. There are various ways in which the actual testing is done. Some require the child's active cooperation and some do not.

The child's response to sounds of different loudness and pitch can be tested with a special machine called an audiometer. His response to sound can also be tested with certain sound-producing things (such as noisemakers, bells, whistles, etc.); to human sounds (such as humming, clucking, puckering or lip-smacking, or verbal directions given at varying degrees of loudness); or by the audiologist imitating the sounds the child is making to see if the child notices them.

The methods chosen to test the child will depend on his age and level of functioning; and the evaluation may require several sessions in order to obtain an accurate assessment of his hearing.

Language and Speech Evaluation

The concern of the speech pathologist in this evaluation is with assessing the child's ability to understand and/or use words, phrases, or sentences. Some of this is done through the use of certain pictures and objects.

The speech pathologist asks himself certain basic questions: Does the child seem to see and hear well? Can he understand what is said to him but is not using speech appropriate for his age? Or does he also have difficulty understanding what is said to him?

It is important to determine the child's ability to deal with certain concepts, such as space, size, shape, and color, because all of these concepts affect his ability to communicate. In this part of the evaluation certain toys, such as puzzles and stack rings, are often used. There is also interest in what kind of a memory the child has for his age and what his general behavior is like.

Since certain kinds of motor development are necessary in order for speech to occur, many areas of the child's functioning are explored, either through parent interview or by direct observation of the child. Examples are how he does in other motor areas (walking, jumping, holding toys); how well he is able to chew, to swallow, to feed himself; whether he can dress or undress himself at all (depending, of course, on his age). The functioning of the parts of the mouth needed for speech are observed: the lips, the tongue, the palate (or roof of the mouth).

All of this is necessary in order to decide if speech therapy is needed and, if so, what its focus will be.

Eye Examination

To be sure that the child's problems are not being complicated by difficulty in seeing, a general eye examination should be part of any diagnostic work-up. The kinds of things which are evaluated in the preschool child are as follows:

acuity — just exactly how well the child can and cannot see; is he near-sighted or far-sighted; does he have cataracts; and so on.

motility — the ability of the muscles that control the eye movements to work efficiently.

binocularity — the ability of the eyes to work together; do the eyes "cross" all the time or only in certain situations; does one eye "turn in" or "turn out," etc.

If glasses are necessary, they can be worn by babies as young as one or two years old. So, again, if a child has a visual problem and it can be treated very early, other problems later on may be prevented or at least be less serious.

Nursing evaluation

Particularly when the child is a preschooler, a meeting between the parents and the public health nurse can be very helpful. The nurse is interested in how the child is doing in the self-help areas and in how the parents can work with the child in areas of his difficulty. For instance, if he cannot feed himself, the nurse may have many ideas about how to prepare the food, what kinds of utensils to make to fit his hands, how to get him to drink out of a cup if he cannot yet sit up, and so on.

The general physical care of the baby is discussed. The nurse may even plan a home visit, if that seems helpful to the parents, in order to demonstrate some of the techniques that the parents would find useful.

If a child requires a lot of physical care, the public health nurse can arrange for a visiting nurse to assist the mother in home care.

Nutrition Evaluation

Since many brain damaged babies are feeding problems and sometimes cannot eat regular table food, the help of the nutritionist may be needed in order to plan meals which the baby can eat and which will give him the nourishment he needs in order to be physically healthy. This evaluation, then, is really an informal conversation with the parents rather than the child. The child's physical condition and medical history, however, are carefully noted.

The nutritionist is also a specialist in how to buy the most nourishing foods on a limited budget; how to serve food in a more appetizing way; and how to plan meals which will insure that the whole family can have a well-balanced diet.

Educational Evaluation

This evaluation is one of the most important in the total work-up because it is concerned with planning for the child's placement in the best available program. The word "education" means different things to different people; I use it here to mean a concern with the formation of the *total* child, physically, socially, emotionally, intellectually, and morally.

The educational evaluation is done by an education specialist who determines the necessary tests to be administered to a child.

These may include standardized tests which evaluate all the areas of the child's functioning that influence his ability to learn.

There are, however, many instances in which children cannot be evaluated by using standardized tests. In these cases diagnostic teaching (observing the child in a learning situation) is used in order to (1) detect possible impairment in the child's sensory ability (how he uses his eyes, how he listens, how he speaks, how he uses his body) and (2) observe the strengths and weaknesses which will assist or delay him in acquiring future learning.

(I would like to say a word here about *play*. We grown-ups tend to see the young child's play activity as frivolous, something he does to keep himself occupied when he has nothing better or more exciting to do. Actually, playing gives the youngster the foundation for *all* of his future learning. In order to play with certain toys, or to play well with other children, a young child must learn certain skills.

Play is one of the most meaningful parts of the preschooler's life. When a child is in a nursery-type program, parents will sometimes say, "All he does there is *play*." His playing is a *wonderful* thing; it is the child who does not, or cannot, play for whom we have extra concern.)

What results from this kind of educational evaluation is a determination of the young child's developmental levels in areas such as motor ability, communication, use of play materials, personal care, and relationships with people. In handicapped youngsters, these developmental levels will be less consistent than in normal children.

The ways in which the handicapped child is tested, even the test materials that are used, depend on the individual child being seen.

The goal of the educational evaluation is not to arrive at a formal diagnosis but, rather, to look at the child's *learning potential* and to determine if a program can be found which will (1) fit the child's needs, (2) let the child start at whatever general level he is on at the moment, (3) allow the child to be in a group where the others are, *as nearly as possible,* on the same functioning and age levels, (4) allow the child to grow educationally, and (5) still be able to meet the child's educational needs in six months or a year.

The Informing Interview

After all the tests and evaluations have been done, the parents are anxious to hear the results. Generally one of the medical doctors (but often several members of the diagnostic team) will go over all of the team's findings with the parents. The parents will receive the team's decisions as to what the basic problem is, what has caused it (if that is known), how the child is functioning, and what the prognosis (outlook for the future) is.

Then the treatment plan is outlined, and the parents decide if they agree with all that's been said and with what is recommended in the way of treatment. Treatment may be carried out at the same center or arranged for at other places. Return visits for reevaluations at specified times may also be planned.

This is the time for the parents to ask questions, to be sure that they understand all that has been said to them, and to be sure that they have a good picture of what their child is doing and not doing (and why), as well as what and how he can be helped to do better.

Chapter 9

SEEKING RESOURCES

M ANY parents may notice that their baby is developing slowly but are not sure just what is the cause. For them, it may be more practical to start out by going to an agency which offers general help and then work up to a specialized agency.

The main reason for this is that the specialized evaluation centers or nursery programs often have waiting lists. It is a terrible disappointment for parents to wait and wait for an appointment and then to find out that they are at the wrong agency. So parents may save valuable time in the long run by letting professional people guide them along the way to the agency that can best serve their child's needs.

The Family Doctor

Certainly a trusted family doctor, if available, should help parents by telling them, to the best of his knowledge, what he thinks is wrong with the baby. He should then encourage them to seek specialized services.

Many doctors keep lists of hospital clinics and community agencies that are available in the local area. If, because of location, there are no agencies readily available, visits to various specialists may be recommended; and the doctor generally has particular people in mind that he would want to send the family to.

Local Health Departments

The local health department is aware of just about every medical and social service that is available in a community.

Public health nurses who work with the child health clinics of the health department are sometimes available to make home visits if it is difficult for the family to travel. The nurse can be very helpful in getting specific services because she will be able to make certain judgments about the child's problems just by seeing the child and talking to the parents. Whatever the problem, the nurse will be glad to help the family make contact with the necessary agency or diagnostic center.

Community Councils

Most large cities and counties have a coordinating agency. It might be called the Community Council, or the United Fund, or the like; or it might be referred to as the local "Red Feather" agency. One of its functions is to keep a listing of all the service agencies (including hospital clinics) in the surrounding area.

The community coordinating agency does not service the child itself but refers the family to a specialized agency. This means the parents have to have in mind the kind of service that they want. Or, if the family is not certain how to begin, it can ask the coordinating agency to recommend the most local *family agency*.

Family Agencies

A general family service agency is available to talk with *any* member of a family about *any* kind of problem. The family agency worker (usually a social worker) can help the parents to determine what their child's specific problem is or what is the best place to go to for diagnosis and treatment.

Specialized Centers or Clinics

Most large hospitals have outpatient clinics which specialize in various kinds of problems. The word *clinic* does not imply that the service is only for poor people; families are generally charged according to their incomes.

Pediatric clinics are usually a good place to start when seeking general help pertaining to a child. In the community there are Keep-Well Stations or Well-Baby Clinics that can serve the same function as the pediatric clinic within the hospital.

From there, the pediatrician can refer the child to other, more specialized parts of a hospital for evaluations or treatment. Not all hospitals have all kinds of specialized services; one hospital may have a mental retardation clinic, another a cerebral palsy clinic, another a muscular dystrophy clinic, and so on.

State Departments

When the family does not live near any specialized services, and is willing to travel within the state to get help, one of the state's departments of health or welfare (it may be the Department of Social Welfare, the Department of Mental Health, the Bureau of Children's Services, etc.) can give general information about state-supported services all over the state. It may even have listings of community-supported or private facilities.

Sometimes the state agency will help the family get to another, more appropriate agency by making an initial contact for them. Especially in emergency situations, the state agencies can be extremely helpful.

The main offices of state departments are generally located in the state capitol.

The Federal Government

The part of the federal government that is devoted exclusively to concerns about children and their problems is called the Children's Bureau, located in Washington, D.C. It is part of the United States Department of Health, Education, and Welfare.

The Children's Bureau not only keeps lists of specialized services but publishes a great many pamphlets and booklets on particular problems of children. These pamphlets are available from the U.S. Government Printing Office, Washington, D.C.

One way of knowing what is happening on the national level is to get on the mailing list of the U.S. Government Printing Office so that any new material that is published can be sent for right away. (Since the Children's Bureau gives grants for research and training as well as for services, and also coordinates what is going on in all the states, many professionals use the Printing Office's publications lists in order to keep up to date.)

For military personnel only, information on programs, agencies, and facilities for the handicapped in communities where the military family lives or may be moving to, can be obtained from the Office of the Surgeon General, Denver, Colorado.

National Organizations

There are specific national organizations, with many local chapters, which are devoted to just about every kind of problem that exists. Following is a list of some of the ones that might be of service to families with babies who are developing slowing.

> The Alexander Graham Bell Association for the Deaf, Inc.
> The Volta Bureau
> 1537 35th Street, N.W.
> Washington, D.C. 20007

> An information center on deafness, with a complete list of preschool and other programs for the deaf. This center has the world's finest library on deafness and has educational programs for parents of deaf children.

> American Foundation for the Blind
> Box FH, 15 West 16 Street
> New York, New York 10011

> Although mostly concerned with blind people of potentially normal intelligence, may be helpful in locating resources for multiply-handicapped blind youngsters in the United States and Canada.

> American Speech and Hearing Association
> 9030 Old Georgetown Road
> Washington, D.C. 20014

> Provides information on evaluation and treatment centers for people with speech and/or hearing disorders.

Association for Children with Learning Disabilities
(formerly the Association for Brain Injured Children)
2200 Brownsville Road
Pittsburgh, Pennsylvania 15210

The coordinating agency for the state and local associations of the same name; also has reading lists for parents of children with minimal brain dysfunction.

Council for Exceptional Children
1411 South Jefferson David Highway
Suite 900
Arlington, Virginia 22202

Concerned with all children who are "exceptional" in the sense of being different from the average child.

Epilepsy Foundation of America
1828 L Street, N.W.
Washington, D.C. 20036

A referral and coordinating agency for all local services for people with epilepsy; also very involved with public education, publishing many pamphlets and booklets on epilepsy.

Muscular Dystrophy Associations of America, Inc.
1790 Broadway
New York, New York 10019

Concerned with research into the cause and cure of muscular dystrophy; through local affiliates, offers educational, recreational, medical, and social services to the dystrophic patient and his family.

National Association for Retarded Children
420 Lexington Avenue
New York, New York 10017

The coordinating agency for all the state and local

associations that service the mentally retarded; also keeps up-to-date lists on diagnostic centers in all the states and publishes factsheets and booklets on mental retardation; local chapters run programs such as nurseries, sheltered workshops, recreation programs, and counselling services for the retardate and his family.

National Easter Seal Society for Crippled
  Children and Adults
2023 West Ogden Avenue
Chicago, Illinois 60612

Through local affiliates, offers consultation, information, and referral services to physically disabled children and adults.

National Foundation — March of Dimes
Public Education Department
Box 2000
White Plains, New York 10602

Concerned with birth defects, their prevention and treatment; keeps an up-to-date list of genetic counselling centers throughout the United States.

National Society for the Prevention of Blindness
79 Madison Avenue
New York, New York 10016

Works with all kinds of community agencies to plan sight conservation programs; sponsors research in eye diseases causing blindness.

Planned Parenthood
Box S, 810 Seventh Avenue
New York, New York 10022

Referral service for information on sterilization, abortion, and birth control.

President's Committee on Mental Retardation
Washington, D.C. 20201

A clearing-house for information on mental retardation services across the country; publishes many pamphlets on mental retardation; is doing much in the way of public education about this handicap.

Social Security Administration
Baltimore, Maryland 21235

Has information concerning social security benefits for the handicapped. All questions are generally handled by local district offices, listed in all telephone directories under the heading, "United States Government, Department of Health, Education, and Welfare."

United Cerebral Palsy Associations, Inc.
66 East 34 Street
New York, New York 10016

A clearing-house for information pertaining to cerebral palsy; also provides local services such as nursery programs, physical therapy, speech therapy, etc.

Chapter 10

WHAT COUNSELLING IS ABOUT

"COUNSELLING" is a word that is used a lot, both by professionals and by families. Some people fear it, others welcome it, depending on what they think the word means. I use it here in its broadest sense, to mean that which takes place between a professional person and a parent or other family member in *any* discussion that has to do with the baby's problem. It can vary from a simple, one-time discussion about how or where to get services for the child, to a lengthy and deeply involved therapy program when assistance is needed in handling the many stresses presented by the child with a handicap.

Counselling is not a thing to be feared or to be ashamed of. All of us, at various times in our lives, come upon problems which for us, at that moment, are just too upsetting or confusing for us to be able to resolve all by ourselves.

We are asking for "counselling" any time we "pour out our hearts" to a friend or relative; or seek advice from someone we respect; or read an article or a book that we think can answer a particular question; or ask someone to just listen to what's on our mind so that we can clear up our thinking. And any time another person comes to us in these ways, he or she is asking for our "counsel."

When it comes to certain kinds of problems, those that involve our deepest emotions, it is often better to seek counselling from a person who is not too close to us, or related to us, or who might be emotionally involved in the situation. That is why a professional person, with special training in how to talk with people about what they are thinking and feeling, is really the best person to go to.

There are a lot of different people who are specialists in certain areas of counselling. For instance, if you want to discuss a medical problem and all of its implications, then of course a medical doctor is the best person for that.

If, after you understand all the medical aspects, you feel that the medical problem is affecting the family in certain ways (perhaps in terms of its cost, or its affect on a marriage, for instance), you then move on to a person who can deal with those other aspects.

That person might be a social worker, a psychologist, or a psychiatrist. Or, for people who feel there is a spiritual aspect to a problem, there is a clergyman. These people are trained to look at the family as a whole, and at each person as part of a family. They can help a person to see all sides of a problem.

When there is a child with a developmental problem which causes certain other problems for the family (upset, fear, shame, need for treatment services, desire for evaluations, etc.), then the best person to talk it all out with is a specialist like those listed above but who has a further specialty of working with families in which there is a handicapped member. Why? Well, because by meeting with and talking to many, many families who go through all kinds of experiences related to having a handicapped member, these specialists have the advantage of being "tuned in" to the special needs of such families.

These specialists know a lot about the medical aspects of handicaps, the different kinds of feelings that people have in general about handicaps, the services that may be needed or that are available in the community, the kinds of behavior that certain handicaps will cause in a child, and so on.

They know how parents might feel when told their child is handicapped; they know how to help parents decide whether to keep a child home, to seek a residential placement, or to try to get a school program. They know how to help a set of parents look at the needs of *every* member of the family. They know the kinds of information that families need in order to be able to make necessary decisions.

Specialists in the field of the handicapped know that there are certain times of "crisis" where the family of the handicapped child is concerned: when the diagnosis is given; when the child gets ready for school; when the child gets toward adolescence; when adulthood is coming along; and when long-range plans must be made. At these times the family may need to have someone to talk to. Someone who *understands.*

The important thing, then, is to be able to find someone who knows about the problem, is not emotionally involved in it, but who understands what the family is going through.

That's asking a lot, even of a professional person.

Many families may tell you they've had some pretty bad experiences with professional people to whom they went with high hopes. Of course there is always the personal element. You have to feel comfortable with the person you're talking to. You have to like him and respect him in order to be able to thrash out some of the most upsetting things, and in order to accept from him some things you might not really want to hear at all, even if they are true.

Professionals, like all other kinds of people, come in a lot of different sizes, shapes, and personalities. Although all of us who deal with the problems of the handicapped are supposed to be dedicated to helping the family work out the best solution to its own problems, we are not always that objective.

Some of us have our own ideas about what a family should do, and we try to convince the family of what *we* think is best. Some of us, who may have different religious beliefs from the family, may be unable to deal properly with the spiritual crises that may arise. Some of us may have days in which we just can't seem to act with the patience and understanding and time that is needed by the family. Some of us simply don't seem to hit it off with certain people, or they with us.

That is all right. It's reality. Knowing these things, the family looking for help should not be discouraged but should feel even more secure about going on looking until it finds a person whom it feels meets all of its needs and with whom it can develop a counselling relationship that is satisfactory and constructive.

By this I do *not* mean just the kind of thing where the professional person says only what he thinks the family wants to hear, or agrees with anything the family says, even if it is not sound.

A good counsellor will sometimes have to help a family to talk about things which are very painful and upsetting and which are perhaps very hard to face or to talk about. Yet, if it is necessary in order for the family to move on to a healthy and good resolution of its problems, then that family will have been lucky to find a good counselling situation. This can all be done with compassion, with care, and with understanding.

Perhaps it will help if I can give some concrete examples of what I am talking about. Let's go back a minute to one of the "crisis" times I mentioned earlier and look at it as a possible time for counselling.

Many families quite frankly say that the greatest upset, the greatest impact, was at the time they received the diagnosis that their child was handicapped. That is the time, many of them tell us, when they would have welcomed so much someone reaching out to them, someone who could have helped them to struggle through those first days, or first weeks, of heartbreak.

We know that very often parents go through what we call a "grief reaction" upon receiving the diagnosis. It is almost like what a parent goes through if a child dies. The difference is that with death we are free to cry, to grieve, then to slowly adjust to that unchangeable fact of death, and finally to get past it and go on.

But when the child is handicapped, we have to deal not only with the actual fact of the handicap, but with all of the other things that will come later on as a direct result of it. The grief, when it comes, is not so easy to get past. It goes on and on, changing and bringing new and other problems to grapple with and to adjust to. It lasts a lifetime.

Because there are so many reasons (some known, most unknown) for a handicap occurring, parents have to deal not only with their grief but also with their fear that in some way they may have caused the child's problem. "What did I do wrong?" so many mothers have asked me. "Was it the virus I had?" "Was it because I fell in my seventh month?" "Was God punishing me for something I did that was bad?" "Was it because I really didn't want this child?"

The reality of what having a handicapped baby will mean in terms of the future can also be upsetting to the parents at the very beginning. They can justly feel angry or resentful or afraid. If they are religious, it may be hard for them to understand God allowing this to happen to them.

It is natural to want to run away from the problem, to ask, "Why did this have to happen to me?" or to say, "The doctor is wrong; this cannot be." In the midst of the initial upset it may seem that there is nothing that can be done for the child *or* for the family.

All of these feelings and reactions I have mentioned, and many I have not, are natural reactions. Parents should feel free to go through them and to be able to talk about them. This is the time when the professional has the greatest obligation to the family, for help at this time can prevent many heartaches later on.

Yet because each family seems to have to go through this time alone, with no previous knowledge that such problems even existed, there is often no one around who can help them when they need help most. There are only a small number of families who even know that help *can* be found.

Without professional help, heartbreaking things can happen, such as parents telling their other children that their hydrocephalic infant died in the hospital and then secretly arranging for exorbitantly expensive private nursing home care; or a mother crying every Monday night for years because Monday was the day of the week that she gave birth to a child with a birth defect; or parents refusing even to see their infant after birth because they do not know what cleft palate or spina bifida or mongolism mean and they are afraid to look at the baby; and so on and on.

It is a sad fact that by the time help comes to many parents, the wounds are too deep. Husbands and wives may somehow have lost each other and their marriage. Sisters and brothers of the baby may be angry and rejecting. Babies who could be at home may be in an institution. Mothers may have been deprived of the joy of caring for and loving babies who need them. And babies who could be growing into productive and useful citizens may not get that help which is so urgently needed in the first few years of their lives.

Many, many families that I have met over the years have experienced the things I have just mentioned. They were people who came in all sizes, shapes, colors, and incomes. Maybe there are as many families with handicapped babies who do not have any problems and do not need help. I don't know them because I have never met them.

The families I *have* met have been able to talk and to share their knowledge, their pain, their fears. And they have reached out to, and helped, other parents because they could truly say, "I understand."

So you see, there is another reason to seek out counselling. Besides getting help for yourself, you can help others who have some of the same problems and who are going through some of the same things. You can learn how to help your neighbors, your friends, your relatives to understand too. In that way you will help us to educate society about handicapped youngsters. Perhaps then the next generation of handicapped babies and their families will not have to go through all the painful things that families go through today.

We have come full circle now. In order for a family to get counselling help, it must know where help is available. In order to look for help, the parents must have some idea about the problem their child has. In order to understand the problem, the family must know what signs to look for and how the problem came about.

These pages have not attempted to take the place of agency help. The very necessary areas of how to handle certain behavior, or how to teach the child to do certain things, have not been touched on. We have not discussed specific medical, educational, or counselling problems in detail. Nor have we dealt with how to handle certain feelings. All of these things would depend on the individual family and the individual child.

What we *have* attempted to do is to gather the kinds of information which can help the family who sees its baby developing slowly, or with difficulty, to take the steps which will lead to the kind of personal and long-term help they will need.

We have tried to pave the way so that families may be spared months, or even years, of despair and frustration in their attempts to get help for themselves and their baby.

And of particular concern have been the babies, to whom time is so precious and for whom the future is now so much more hopeful.

BIBLIOGRAPHY

I. The following books and articles may be of interest to parents who wish to read further about specific developmental handicaps.

An Introduction to Mental Retardation: Problems, Plans and Programs. The Secretary's Comm. on Mental Retardation, U.S. Dept. of Health, Education and Welfare, Washington, D.C., U.S. Govt. Printing Office, June, 1965.

Becker, Wesley C.: Parents Are Teachers: A Child Management Program. Champaign, Research Press, 1971.

Canfield, Norton: You and Your Hearing. Public Affairs Pamphlet No. 315. New York, Public Affairs Comm., 1961.

Cerebral Palsy: What You Should Know About It. New York, United Cerebral Palsy Assns., no date.

Davies, Stanley P.; and Katharine G. Ecob: The Mentally Retarded in Society. New York, Columbia Univ. Press, 1959.

Deibert, Alwin N.; and Alice J. Harmon: New Tools for Changing Behavior. Champaign, Research Press, 1970.

Demary, Helen Curtis: Check Your Child's Eyes. Washington, D.C., Prevention of Blindness Society of Metropolitan Washington, 1962.

Dittman, Laura L.: The Mentally Retarded Child at Home. Children's Bureau Publication No. 374. Washington, D.C., U.S. Govt. Printing Office, 1966.

Egg, Maria: When a Child is Different. New York, John Day, 1964.

Epilepsy: Hope Through Research. U.S. Dept. of Health, Education and Welfare, Washington, D.C., U.S. Govt. Printing Office, 1963. (Also available in Spanish: Epilepsia: Esperanza en la Investigacion, 1964.)

Faber, Nancy W.: The Retarded Child. New York, Crown, 1968.

Facts on Mental Retardation. New York, National Assn. of Retarded Children, 1969.

French, Edward: Child in the Shadows. Philadelphia, Lippincott, 1960.

He LOOKS Like Other Kids, But. . . . Assn. for Children with Learning Disabilities, no date.

Health, Education and Welfare Indicators: Epilepsy. U.S. Dept of Health, Education and Welfare, Washington, D.C., U.S. Govt. Printing Office, Dec., 1964.

Heard, Joseph: Hope Through Doing. New York, John Day, 1968.

Hello World. The President's Comm. on Mental Retardation, Washington, D.C., no date.

Hurley, Rodger L.: Poverty and Mental Retardation: A Causal Relationship. Trenton, State of New Jersey, Dept. of Institutions and Agencies, Div. of Mental Retardation, Planning and Implementation Project, April, 1968.

Illness Among Children: Data from U.S. National Health Survey. Children's Bureau, U.S. Dept. of Health, Education and Welfare, Washington, D.C., U.S. Govt. Printing Office, 1963.

Jacobs, Jerry: The Search for Help. New York, Brunner, Mazel, 1969.

Keats, Sydney: Cerebral Palsy. Springfield, Thomas, 1965.

Kennedy, John F.: Message from the President of the United States Relative to Mental Illness and Mental Retardation. Document No. 58, 86th Congress, First Session, House of Representatives, Feb. 5, 1963.

Kirk, Samuel; Merle B. Karnes; and Winifred D. Kirk: You and Your Retarded Child. Palo Alto, Pacific Books, 1968.

Learning Disabilities Due to Minimal Brain Dysfunction: Hope Through Research, revised ed. National Institute of Health Publication No. 211. U.S. Dept. of Health, Education and Welfare, Washington, D.C., U.S. Govt. Printing Office, 1968.

Levinson, Abraham: The Mentally Retarded Child; A Guide for Parents. New York, John Day, 1952.

Lewis, Richard S.; Alfred A. Strauss; and Laura E. Lehtinen: The Other Child. New York, Grune & Stratton, 1960.

Lin-Fu, Jane S.: Lead Poisoning in Children. Children's Bureau Publication No. 452. U.S. Dept. of Health, Education and Welfare, Washington, D.C., U.S. Govt. Printing Office, 1967.

Loewy, Herta: The Retarded Child: A Guide for Parents and Teachers. New York, Philosophical Library, 1951.

New Approaches to Mental Illness and Mental Retardation. Secretary's Comm. on Mental Retardation, U.S. Dept. of Health, Education and Welfare, Washington, D.C., U.S. Govt. Printing Office, 1963.

O'Neill, John J.: The Hard of Hearing. Englewood Cliffs, Prentice-Hall, 1964.

Semple, Jean E.: Hearing Impaired Pre-School Child. Springfield, Thomas, 1970.

Sheets, Boyd V.: Helping the Patient with Cerebral Palsy to Communicate. New York, United Cerebral Palsy Assns, 1967.

Siegel, Ernest: Helping the Brain-Injured Child: A Handbook for Parents. New York Assn. for Brain Injured Children, 1961.

Slaughter, Stella: The Mentally Retarded Child and His Parents. New York, Harper & Row, 1960.

Smith, Bert Kruger: Your Nonlearning Child. Boston, Beacon Press, 1968.

Spock, Benjamin: Baby and Child Care, revised ed. New York, Pocket Books, 1967.

Stuart, Mark A.; and George James: The Unprotected: A Five-Part Report on Child Abuse. Hackensack, The Record, Nov., 1970.

Summaries of Articles on Juvenile Epilepsy. Epilepsy Foundation, Parke, Davis & Co., 1967.

The Pre-School Child Who is Blind. Children's Bureau Folder No. 39-1953. U.S. Dept. of Health, Education and Welfare, Washington, D.C., U.S. Govt. Printing Office, 1953.

Theodore, Sister Mary, O.S.F.: The Challenge of the Retarded Child. Milwaukee, Bruce, 1963.

Viscardi, Henry, Jr.: The Abilities Story. New York, Erickson, 1967.

Wood, Maxine: Blindness — Ability, not Disability, revised ed. Public Affairs Pamphlet No. 295A. New York, Public Affairs Comm., Inc., 1968.

You, Your Child and Epilepsy. Washington, D.C., Epilepsy Foundation of America, 1968.

Your Child From One to Six, revised ed. Children's Bureau Publication No. 30. U.S. Dept. of Health, Education and Welfare, Washington, D.C., U.S. Govt. Printing Office, 1959.

II. Additional background reading for this book.

Anastasi, Anne: Psychological Testing, 2nd ed. New York, Macmillan, 1961.

Baumeister, Alfred A. (Ed.): Mental Retardation: Appraisal, Education, Rehabilitation. Chicago, Aldine, 1967.

Berko, Frances: Management of Brain Damaged Children. Springfield, Thomas, 1970.

Berry, Mildred Freburg: Language Disorders of Children: The Bases and Diagnoses. New York, Appleton-Century-Crofts, 1969.

A Program for Aphasic Children. Reprint No. 851. Washington, D.C., Volta Bureau, 1966.

Casework Services for Parents of Handicapped Children. Ten papers reprinted from Social Casework. New York, Family Service Assn. of America, no date.

Chaney, Mrs. W. Arthur: Vocabulary of Terms Used in Perceptual Motor Training. Santa Ana, Orange County Chapter, Calif. Assn. for Neurologically Impaired Children, no date.

Critchley, Macdonald: The Dyslexic Child, 2nd ed. Springfield, Thomas, 1970.

Facts About Lead and Pediatrics. New York, Lead Industries Assn., 1969.

Farber, Bernard R.: Mental Retardation: Its Social Context and Social Consequences. Boston, Houghton Mifflin, 1968.

Feeding Mentally Retarded Children: A Guide for Nurses Working with Families Who have Mentally Retarded Children. Children's Bureau, U.S. Dept. of Health, Education and Welfare, Washington, D.C., U.S. Govt. Printing Office, 1964.

Frampton, Merle E.; and Elena Gall (Eds.): Special Education for the Exceptional, Volume II: The Physically Handicapped and Special Health Problems, 2nd printing. Boston, Porter Sargent, 1960.

Gustafson, Sarah R. (Ed.): The Pediatric Patient: 1964. Philadelphia, Lippincott.

Gustafson, Sarah R. (Ed.): The Pediatric Patient: 1965. Philadelphia, Lippincott.

Haynes, Una: The Role of Nursing in Programs for Patients with Cerebral Palsy and Related Disorders. New York, United Cerebral Palsy Assns., Inc., 1962.

Jersild, Arthur T.: Child Psychology, 5th ed. Englewood Cliffs, Prentice-Hall, 1960.

Kanner, Leo: A History of the Care and Study of the Mentally Retarded. Springfield, Thomas, 1964.

Kessler, Jane W.: Psychopathology of Childhood. Englewood Cliffs, Prentice-Hall, 1966.

Levinson, Abraham; and John A. Bigler: Mental Retardation in Infants and Children. Chicago Year Book Publishers, 1960.

Teaching Aphasic Children. Reprint No. 677. Washington, D.C., Volta Bureau, no date.

Martmer, Edgar E. (Ed.): The Child With a Handicap: A Team Approach to His Care and Guidance. Springfield, Thomas, 1959.

Mental Retardation: A Handbook for the Primary Physician. A report of the American Medical Association Conference on Mental Retardation, Chicago, April 9-11, 1964. (Manuscript prepared by Cathy Covert.)

Minimal Brain Dysfunction: A New Problem Area for Social Work. Chicago, National Easter Seal Society for Crippled Children, 1968.

Morris, William (Ed.): The American Heritage Dictionary of the English Language. New York, American Heritage, Houghton Mifflin, 1969.

Myklebust, Helmer R.: Auditory Disorders in Children: A Manual for Differential Diagnosis. New York, Grune & Stratton, 1954.

Resuscitation of the Newborn. The Special Comm. on Infant Mortality of the Medical Society of the County of New York, 1963.

Schreiber, Meyer (Ed.): Social Work and Mental Retardation. New York, John Day, 1970.

The Six-Hour Retarded Child. U.S. Dept. of Health, Education and Welfare, Washington, D.C., U.S. Govt. Printing Office, 1969.

Stedman's Medical Dictionary, 21st ed. Baltimore, Williams & Wilkins, 1966.

Taber, Clarence Wilbur: Taber's Cyclopedic Medical Dictionary, 9th ed. Philadelphia, F.A. Davis, 1963.

The Role of the Ophthalmologist in Dyslexia. Melbourne, Fla., Institute for Development of Educational Activities, Inc., 1969.

Wolf, James M. (Ed.): The Blind Child With Concomitant Disabilities. Research Series No. 16. New York, American Foundation for the Blind, 1967.

INDEX

A

Abused child, 19
Aggressiveness, 29
Amblyopia, 34
Amino acid, 14, 50, 53
Amniocentesis, 22-23, 50
Amniotic fluid, 20, 22, 50
Anoxia, 16, 51
Apgar Score, 24, 51
Aphasia, 51
Audiologist, 56, 64
Auditory nerves, 35
Autism, 44, 51
Awkwardness, 29

B

Bacterial infections, 12
"Battered baby", 19
Behavior modification, 51
Birth injuries, 16
Blindness, 10, 40
 functional, 32
 legal, 32
Blood type, 13
Brain, 11-12, 51
 inflammation of, 18
Brain damage, 11, 12-19, 21-26, 27, 51
 after birth, 17-19
 at birth, 16-17
 before birth, 12-16
 characteristics of, 27-30
 prevention of, 21-26
Brain injured, 37
Brain injury, 51
Breech delivery, 17, 52

C

Central nervous system, 11-12, 52

dysfunction, 27
 impairment, 27
Cerebral palsy, 10, 19, 31, 40, 44-45, 52
Child abuse, 19
Chromosome, 14, 52
 abnormalities, 14
Chronological age, 52
Coma, 17, 49, 52
Congenital, 52
Consanguinity, 20
Convulsions, 17, 46-48
Convulsive disorder, 18-19
Counselling, 76-81
 genetic, 23, 56
Craniostenosis, 14
Cretinism, 14
Cyanosis, 52
Cystic fibrosis, 3, 14, 52

D

Destructiveness, 29
Diagnostic evaluation, 58-68
Disability, 4
Distractibility, 28
Down's syndrome, 55
Drugs, 15, 17
Dyslexia, 37, 53

E

Early childhood development, 7-9
Echolalia, 53
Echopraxia, 53
Educable retarded, 42
Educational evaluation, 66-67
EEG, *see* Electroencephalogram
Electroencephalogram, 38, 47, 53
Encephalitis, 18, 33, 53
Endocrinologist, 56
Enzyme, 53

Epilepsy, 10, 46-48
Eye examination, 65

F

Febrile convulsions, 47, 48
Fetal position, 17
Fetus, 13, 18, 53

G

Genes, 14, 52, 54
Genetic counselling, 23, 56
Geneticist, 56
German measles, 18
  see also Rubella
Grand mal seizures, 47

H

Handicap, definition of, 4
Handicaps, prevention of, 21-26
Hearing evaluation, 63-64
Hearing problems, 34-35
Heredity, 14, 54
Hydrocephalus, 14, 31
Hyperactivity, 17, 28, 38

I

Immaturity, 29
Impairment, 4
Impulsiveness, 28
Infantile autism, *see* Autism
Informing interview, 68
Intake interview, 59-60
Intelligence test, 54
Intra-uterine diagnosis, 23
I.Q., 54, 62-63
Irritability, 28, 29

K

Karyotype, 52

L

Language evaluation, 64-65
Language disorder, 54

Language problems, 34, 35-37
"Lazy eye", 34
Lead poisoning, 18, 25, 33, 48-49
  see also Plumbism
Learning disabilities, 37

M

Malnutrition, 24
Measles, 18, 33
  see also Rubeola
Meningitis, 18, 33, 54
Mental age, 54, 63
Mental illness, 40, 44, 54
Mental retardation, 10, 13, 16, 40-44
  definition of, 41
  mild, 42
  moderate, 42-43
  profound, 42, 43
  severe, 42, 43
Metabolic disorders, 13-14, 54
Microcephaly, 14
Minimal brain dysfunction, 37-39
Mongolism, *see* Down's syndrome
Multiply-handicapped, 4, 45
Muscular dystrophy, 10, 31, 40, 45-46

N

Nerves, 11-12, 55
Neurologically impaired, 37
Neurological evaluation, 61
Neurologist, 56
Neurosurgeon, 56
Nursing evaluation, 65-66
Nutrition, 15, 18
Nutrition evaluation, 66
Nutritionist, 56, 66

O

Obstetrician, 56
Operant conditioning, *see* Behavior
  modification
Ophthalmia neonatorum, 32
Ophthalmologist, 56
Optometrist, 56
Organic brain damage, 27
Organic impairment, 27

Orthopedic problems, 31-32
Orthopedist, 56
Otologist, 56

P

Parasitic infections, 12
Pediatrician, 56, 58
Perceptual problems, 38
Perceptually impaired, 37
Peripheral nervous system, 52
Perseveration, 30
Petit mal seizures, 47
Phenylketonuria, 14, 23, 55
Physiatrist, 57
Physical examination, 60-61
Physical therapist, 57
Pica, 55
PKU, *see* Phenylketonuria
Placenta, 12
Play, 67
Plumbism, 48
    see also Lead poisoning
Poverty, 24-26
Prematurity, 15, 16, 55
Prenatal diagnosis, 23
Projective tests, 62
Prognosis, 55, 68
Protein deficiency, 15, 18
Psychiatric evaluation, 63
Psychiatrist, 57, 63
Psychoanalyst, 57
Psychological evaluation, 61-63
Psychological test, 54
Psychologist, 57

Public health nurse, 57

R

Retrolental fibroplasia, 33
Rh problem, 13, 23
Rubella, 12, 18, 33
    see also German measles
Rubeola, 18
    see also Measles

S

Seizure, 18, 46
    see also Convulsions
Sickle cell anemia, 3, 13, 54, 55
"Six hour retardate", 42
Social age, 63
Social worker, 57
Speech evaluation, 64
Speech development, 34, 36
Speech pathologist, 57
Speech problems, 4, 30, 35-37

T

Tay-Sachs disease, 3, 57
Toxemia, 12, 14, 16
Toxoplasmosis, 12, 33, 57
Trainable retarded, 42-43

V

Visual problems, 32-34